MOTORSPORTS ENCYCLOPEDIAS

THE MUSCLE CARS ENCYCLOPEDIA

BY KRISTIN J. RUSSO

Encyclopedias

An Imprint of Abdo Reference
abdobooks.com

TABLE OF CONTENTS

THE HISTORY OF MUSCLE CARS 4
UNDER THE HOOD 14
ICONIC MUSCLE CARS 20
AMERICAN MOTORS CORPORATION 24
BUICK 34
CHEVROLET 42
DODGE 72
FORD 90
MERCURY 116
OLDSMOBILE 126
PLYMOUTH 134

PONTIAC 152	**MODERN MUSCLE CARS** 180
CULTURE 172	**GLOSSARY** 188
RACING 174	**TO LEARN MORE** 189
CUSTOMIZATION 176	**INDEX** 190
CAR SHOWS 178	**PHOTO CREDITS** 191

THE HISTORY OF MUSCLE CARS

Muscle cars of the late 1960s and early 1970s are known for their power, fast acceleration, and engines that roar. But muscle cars are much more than just vehicles. They are symbols of style, freedom, and independence. They have become a part of American history and culture.

The height of the classic muscle car era was in the 1960s and early 1970s, but the history of the muscle car begins earlier. In the late 1940s and early 1950s, carmakers competed to build powerful cars. In 1949, the car manufacturer Oldsmobile introduced the Rocket 88. This car was special. Its engine, called the Rocket V-8, had 135 horsepower. It was more powerful than other engines at that time.

The Rocket 88 became a popular car. It accelerated quickly and hit high speeds. People also liked its smooth and sleek design. The Rocket 88 began a new trend for faster cars with more powerful engines.

FLEX YOUR KNOWLEDGE

The term "muscle car" wasn't used until the 1960s. Like muscles, these cars' engines were known to be strong.

1949 Oldsmobile Rocket 88

In the 1950s, carmakers began making more cars with powerful V-8 engines. And then in 1964, the Pontiac GTO rolled off the assembly line. The idea behind building a muscle car was to put the largest engine possible into the lightest possible car body. This would make the car go fast. And that's exactly what the GTO did.

The GTO became popular with the Baby Boomer generation, people who were born between 1946 and 1964. In the mid-1960s, the first Baby Boomers were starting to drive. They were young and carefree, and they wanted cars that represented freedom, power, and independence. The GTO was just such a car.

FUN FACT
Many consider the GTO to be the first muscle car.

1964 Pontiac GTO

THE HISTORY OF MUSCLE CARS

Soon, other carmakers began making muscle cars. Ford released the Mustang. Even though the first Mustang wasn't a muscle car, it helped pave the way for other, faster cars. Designer and race car driver Carroll Shelby worked on the Mustang. He created the Shelby GT350 and GT500, which are classic muscle cars.

Chevrolet launched the Chevelle Super Sport. Dodge made the Challenger. And Plymouth released the Barracuda. Each new car had its own unique style. But they all had one thing in common: high-powered V-8 engines that made them strong and fast. These special cars launched the famous muscle car era of the 1960s and early 1970s, when fast and strong engines were the most popular cars on the road.

1965 Ford Shelby Mustang GT350

A Chevrolet Chevelle competes in a drag race.

Muscle cars already had bold designs with bright colors. Drivers made their cars more exciting by adding racing stripes and decals, shiny front grilles, and oversized tires.

Thanks to their powerful engines, some muscle cars were awkward and heavy. They were good at speeding in a straight line, but they weren't great at making turns on curvy roads. This made muscle cars popular among drag racers.

FLEX YOUR KNOWLEDGE

In a drag race, two drivers go as fast as possible in a straight line. This is different from other kinds of racing that have laps with turns.

THE HISTORY OF MUSCLE CARS

The Muscle Car era was an exciting time for drag racing. Some drag racers became famous. Bill "Grumpy" Jenkins won races driving Chevrolet cars, such as the Nova and Camaro. Don Nicholson raced muscle cars, which included the Mercury Cougar and the Ford Maverick.

Bob Glidden was well-known in Pro Stock racing during the 1970s. He raced Ford muscle cars and won several racing championships.

Jenkins, Nicholson, Glidden, and others like them showed how fast and strong muscle cars could be. They helped make muscle cars even more popular.

The front wheels of a Chevrolet Chevelle lift off the ground at the start of a drag race.

Steve McQueen drives a 1968 Ford Mustang GT in *Bullitt*.

Suddenly, muscle cars seemed to be everywhere—in the movies, on television, and even in music. Movies like *Bullitt*, *The Fast & Furious*, *Vanishing Point*, and *Dirty Mary, Crazy Larry* feature muscle cars in high-speed chases and doing amazing stunts.

Famous musicians sang about muscle cars. The Beach Boys sang songs like "Little Deuce Coupe" and "409" about hot rods and muscle cars. Bruce Springsteen's 1975 album had songs like "Born to Run" and "Thunder Road." Both songs had lyrics about the fun and thrill of driving. By the 1970s, muscle cars had become important symbols of American culture.

THE HISTORY OF MUSCLE CARS

Muscle cars used a lot of fuel. They were called "gas guzzlers." This was an aspect of muscle cars that many drivers didn't like.

People began to realize that cars that used a lot of gasoline could be bad for the environment. In the early 1970s, gasoline also became very expensive. In some countries, including the United States, an oil embargo made fuel hard to get. People had to wait in long gas lines to fill up their tanks.

New rules and taxes made it more difficult and expensive to own a muscle car. Carmakers made changes to their designs and built cars that used less fuel. By the late 1970s, the classic age of the muscle car was over.

Cars line up to wait for fuel at a gas station in 1979.

    Today, people still love muscle cars because they remind them of the days when cars were simple, strong, and made drivers feel free and rebellious.

    Some car companies have brought back old muscle car models. These new muscle cars are a mix of old-style design and modern power and technology.

    New muscle cars use less fuel. They still focus on being fast and powerful, but they have changed over time to be kinder to the environment. Muscle cars hold a special place in the hearts of people who love their style, power, and performance.

THE HISTORY OF MUSCLE CARS

TIMELINE

1964
Chevrolet made the Chevelle, and Oldsmobile released the 4-4-2 to compete with the GTO and other new muscle cars.

1949
Oldsmobile launched the Rocket 88.

1967
The famous Chevrolet Camaro hit the road.

| 1940s | 1950s | 1960s | 1970s |

1964
Pontiac released the GTO. The term "muscle car" was used for the first time to describe the GTO.

1966
Dodge launched the iconic Charger.

1967
Using the Mustang as a model, Ford designed and released the Shelby GT500.

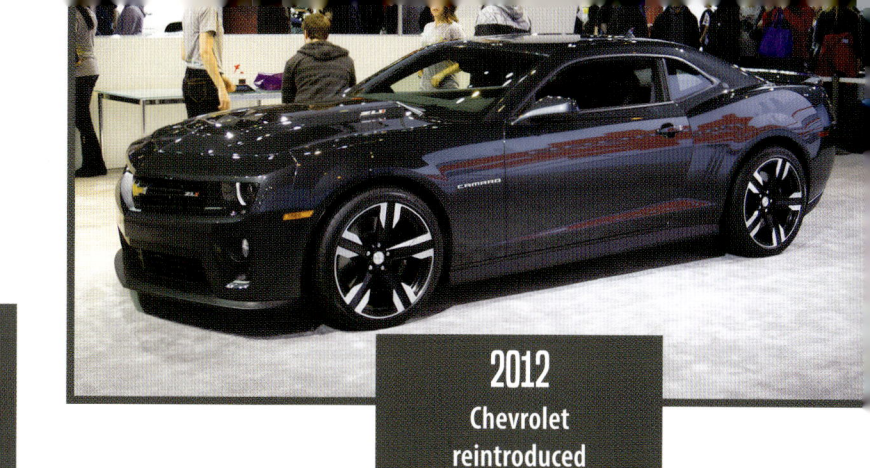

1971–1972
New rules and taxes made it cost more to own cars that used a lot of gas.

2012
Chevrolet reintroduced the Camaro ZL1, a supercharged modern-day muscle car.

1974
The classic Pontiac GTO muscle car model was no longer made.

| 1980s | 1990s | 2000s | 2010s | 2020s |

1973
A worldwide oil shortage created a need for more fuel-efficient cars. Muscle cars became less popular.

13

UNDER THE HOOD

DIAGRAM OF A MUSCLE CAR

There are many parts to a muscle car. Some features enhance power. Others provide additional speed.

HOOD SCOOP: allows air to flow into the engine

ENGINE: powers the car with a strong V-8

GRILLE: gives the car a bold look

1970 DODGE CHALLENGER

FASTBACK ROOF: makes the car aerodynamic

SPOILER: reduces drag to enhance aerodynamics

REAR WHEEL: designed to provide extra traction and speed

BODY: most often a two-door coupe

UNDER THE HOOD

Muscle cars have combustion engines. These engines have parts called cylinders. Each cylinder takes in a mixture of air and gasoline. Once the air and fuel are inside the cylinder, a piston moves up and compresses the mixture.

When the mixture is compressed tightly, a spark plug creates a spark, just like a little lightning bolt. This spark makes a small, controlled explosion inside the cylinder.

The explosion pushes the piston down with a lot of force. The piston's movement, which is connected to the car's wheels, then helps turn the wheels and make the car go.

Inside a combustion engine

A customized V-8 engine

After the explosion, there are some gases that need to be released from the cylinder. When the piston goes back up, the extra gases are pushed out through an exhaust pipe. The engine does this over and over again, very quickly, like a heartbeat. The more times the process repeats over and over, the faster the engine can go.

Many muscle cars also have a hood scoop, a bump with an opening on the hood of the car. The hood scoop is like a special nose for the car. It helps bring air into the car's engine, giving it additional power and speed. Some cars have dual hood scoops to bring in even more air.

UNDER THE HOOD

HOW ARE MUSCLE CARS DIFFERENT?

Muscle cars had V-8 engines. V-8 engines had eight cylinders that spread out at the top and came together at the bottom, in a V-shape. V-8 engines could accelerate quickly in a very short amount of time.

Muscle cars also had a unique type of suspension. Suspension is made up of springs and shock absorbers. In classic muscle cars, these parts were stiffer than those in regular cars. This stiffness helped keep the car steady as it sped up.

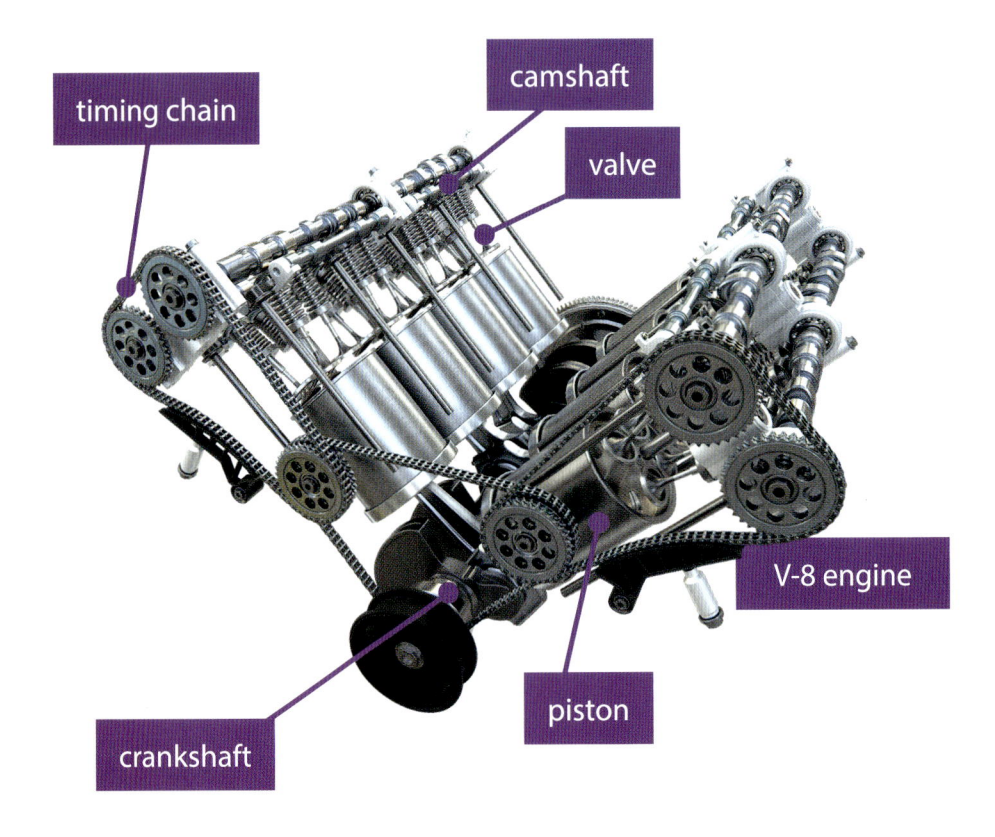

- timing chain
- camshaft
- valve
- V-8 engine
- piston
- crankshaft

1970 Dodge Challenger

    Thanks to a unique exhaust system, muscle cars made a special grumbling sound. The exhaust system made a rumble when the car took off. People liked this deep growling sound.

    Muscle cars had a special look. They were known for having a boxy shape in the front to make room for their large engines. The back ends were smaller, especially if the body type was a two-door coupe. They had bold front grilles on their wide bodies, and many had spoilers, hood scoops, and racing stripes. Cars such as the 1970 Dodge Challenger, 1969 Chevrolet Camaro, and 1976 Pontiac Firebird Trans Am featured the iconic, bold muscle car design styles.

    Unlike modern cars with lots of fancy gadgets, muscle cars kept it simple inside. Most had easy-to-reach controls on user-friendly dashboards. Many thought that one of the best features of muscle cars was their affordability. They were simple, and most focused on power and speed rather than luxury.

ICONIC MUSCLE CARS

All muscle cars are considered to have strong personalities. But some are more memorable than others. These standout cars are some of the most famous in muscle car history.

1968 AMC AMX
The AMX was launched as a way to rebrand AMC's image.

1969 Chevrolet Camaro
The Camaro was built to compete with the Ford Mustang.

1970 Chevrolet Chevelle SS
The 1970 Chevelle was known for its powerful engine.

1965 Chevrolet Impala
In the mid-1960s, the Impala was a widely popular car.

1972 Dodge Challenger
The Dodge Challenger has had many appearances in movies and television shows.

ICONIC MUSCLE CARS

1970 Dodge Super Bee
The Super Bee cost less than many muscle cars of its time.

1968 Ford Mustang
The Ford Mustang had wide appeal among young drivers.

1970 Oldsmobile 4-4-2
The 4-4-2 was built to compete with the Pontiac GTO.

1971 Plymouth Barracuda
The Barracuda was one of the first muscle cars with a fastback design.

1964 Pontiac GTO
Many regard the GTO as the first true muscle car.

1967 Shelby GT500
The Shelby GT500 was designed by famous carmaker Carroll Shelby.

AMERICAN MOTORS CORPORATION

The American Motors Corporation (AMC) was created when two smaller car companies, Nash Motors and Hudson Motor Car Company, joined forces in 1954. AMC made many different kinds of cars.

They had small cars, medium-sized cars, and off-road vehicles that weren't meant for regular city driving. In 1956, AMC produced the Rambler, which was the first modern compact car in the United States. With a small body and a powerful engine, it was like an early muscle car.

QUICK STATS

- **Company Headquarters**: Southfield, Michigan
- **Years of Operation**: 1954 to 1988
- **Best-Selling Muscle Car**: AMX

1950s Nash Metropolitan

FUN FACT

Between 1968 and 1970, AMC produced 19,134 AMX cars.

In the 1960s, AMC wanted to enter the popular muscle car market. They began designing cars that would appeal to new and younger buyers.

In 1967, AMC started making some powerful muscle cars and parts. AMC muscle cars such as the AMX, the Javelin, and the Rebel became popular.

In the 1980s, AMC developed money problems. They found it tough to compete with bigger car companies. In 1987, a company called Chrysler bought AMC. By 1988, AMC cars were no longer made.

1960s Rambler

AMERICAN MOTORS CORPORATION

AMX

The AMX launched in 1968. It was a new design for AMC, which had been known as a company that made economy cars, cars that are inexpensive and efficient, but not always exciting. AMC wanted to create something new that would change its image. The AMX did that. It was a sporty two-seater car with a bold grille and a fastback roof. It looked like a race car.

1970 AMX

FUN FACT

AMX stands for American Motors Experimental. The AMX name was first given to the concept car that was built before it went into production.

QUICK STATS

- **Years Built**: 1968 to 1970
- **Maximum Horsepower**: 325 hp (1970)
- **0 to 60 miles per hour (97 kmh)**: 6.5 seconds

Big Bad AMX in Go Green

Like other muscle cars, the AMX was lightweight and had a small, two-door body. Its compact style meant it could only fit passengers in the front seats. There was very little space in the back.

In 1970, the "Big Bad" AMX 390 became available. It turned out to be the fastest AMC muscle car they ever made. That was not surprising since this car was designed mostly for racing on a straight track.

The Super Stock AMX had a customized "Big Bad" engine that produced more than 400 horsepower. The Super Stock AMX is rare. Only 52 of these cars were made.

FLEX YOUR KNOWLEDGE

The California Special AMC was a version of the AMX 390, designed to be the pace car at the Riverside International Speedway. Copies were sold to the public. It was painted Go Green and had a black racing stripe down the middle.

AMERICAN MOTORS CORPORATION

HURST SC/RAMBLER

With help from Hurst, a company that made high-performance car parts, AMC redesigned the Rambler Rogue to create the Hurst SC/Rambler. The car's full name when it debuted was the AMC SC/Rambler-Hurst, but most people just called it the Scrambler.

To create the car, AMC used a powerful V-8 engine, like the 315-horsepower 390-cubic-inch (6.4 liter) one from the AMX. Engineers added a special four-speed transmission with a Hurst shifter that helped drivers change gears quickly between the engine's four speeds.

QUICK STATS

- **Year Built**: 1969
- **Maximum Hp**: 315 hp (1969)
- **0 to 60 mph (97 kmh)**: 6.3 seconds

1969 AMC Hurst SC/Rambler

All SC/Ramblers started as white cars with special wheels, racing mirrors, a dark front grille and back panel, Hurst badges, and a special hood scoop. Some had extra red-and-blue stripes and graphics, while others had simpler stripes.

FLEX YOUR KNOWLEDGE

Most classic muscle cars could drive a quarter-mile (0.4 km) in about 13 to 14 seconds, and the 1969 SC/Rambler was no different. It could hit the quarter-mile (0.4 km) mark in 14.3 seconds. Modern muscle cars can achieve times in the high 10- to low 12-second range, and customized high-performance models can break into the 9-second range.

AMERICAN MOTORS CORPORATION

JAVELIN

The Javelin was first introduced in August 1967 for the 1968 model year. It was AMC's entry into the "pony car market."

Pony cars are known for their performance and speed, often equipped with powerful engines that provide a driving experience that many consider thrilling. Pony cars are smaller and more affordable than traditional muscle cars. They typically have two doors and a sleek profile.

Although it was considered a pony car, the Javelin had a little more space inside and in the trunk compared to others like it. Even the back seat had more room.

The Javelin came with power steering. Not all cars then did. Cars without power steering are difficult to turn. Drivers need to use a lot of strength. With power steering, the steering wheel can be turned easily.

Bright paint options including neon blue, orange, or green were offered, along with painted bumpers and bumper guards. This was part of AMC's effort to appeal to younger buyers who wanted more exciting colors.

QUICK STATS

- **Years Built:** 1968 to 1974
- **Maximum Hp:** 315 hp (1969)
- **0 to 60 mph (97 kmh):** 7.6 seconds

AMC Javelin

FLEX YOUR KNOWLEDGE

Craig Breedlove was a famous daredevil who broke five world speed records. In 1968, AMC wanted to show off how fast the Javelin could go. They asked Breedlove to race it. He reached a top speed of 161.7 miles (260 km) per hour.

AMERICAN MOTORS CORPORATION

REBEL

In 1957, AMC introduced the Rambler Rebel and coined the "Rebel" name. The Rambler Rebel had a lightweight frame with a powerful engine. It was among the earliest of AMC's muscle cars, though it was not yet called that name.

There were several different versions of the Rebel until 1970, when AMC launched the most iconic Rebel model, called "The Machine." It was launched on the heels of AMC's success with the Hurst SC/Rambler in 1969.

The Machine was famous for its red, white, and blue look. It was painted white with a prominent blue stripe on the hood and had red, white, and blue stripes on the front, sides, and rear.

AMC Rebel Machine

The Rebel was a medium-sized car that also came as a station wagon.

The Machine models had special wheels that were painted to make them look shiny. These wheels were 15 inches (38 cm) wide and 7 inches (18 cm) tall. AMC called them "15-inch styled road wheel" in their ads, but car fans liked to call them "Machine wheels."

The wheels came with a chrome center cap that had a blue trim disc. They had five slots to help cool the brakes. The trim ring didn't cover the edge of the wheel. Weights could be put on the wheel to help balance the car.

QUICK STATS
- **Years Built**: 1957 to 1960; 1966 to 1967; 1967 to 1970
- **Maximum Hp**: 340 hp (1970)
- **0 to 60 mph (97 kmh)**: 6.5 seconds

BUICK

The Buick car company was founded in 1899 by David Dunbar Buick. When cars were first made, many did not have windshields or doors. Buick became one of the first automakers to close in car frames with doors and windows to keep people comfortable and safe inside.

In 1908, Buick became part of a larger company called General Motors. In the 1960s, Buick caught muscle car fever. In 1963, they launched the Riviera. In 1964 and 1965, Buick brought out the Skylark Gran Sport.

In 1970, Buick made the GSX, a faster version of the Skylark GS. It had a big 455-cubic-inch (7.5 l) V-8 engine. And it had a strong, sporty look. This made it one of Buick's most famous muscle cars.

In 1971, new rules about pollution meant Buick and other car companies had to make engines that used less gas. In some cases, this made them less powerful. By 1972, Buick's GS cars were not as fast as they had been.

Today, Buick still makes quality cars. They focus on new technology and sleek designs. They have a reputation for making reliable, comfortable family cars.

QUICK STATS

- **Company Headquarters**: Detroit, Michigan
- **Years of Operation**: 1899 to present
- **Best-Selling Muscle Car**: Skylark GS

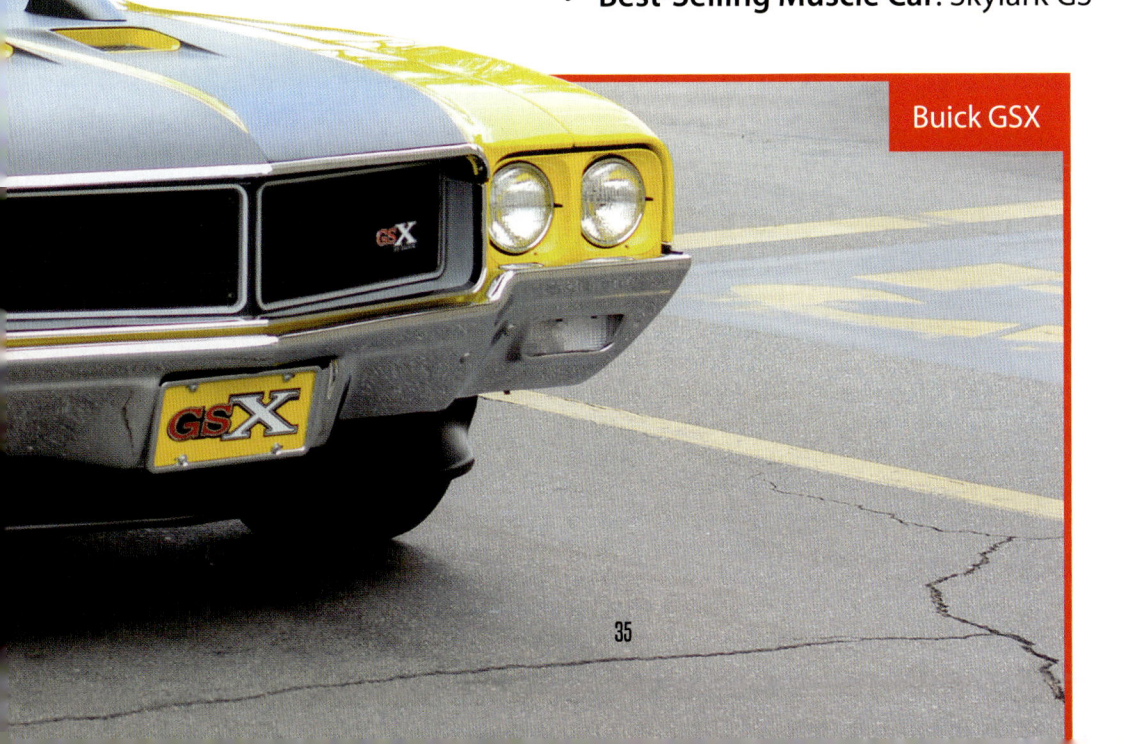

Buick GSX

GRAN SPORT

The Gran Sport was a fancier type of Riviera. At first, it was called the Riviera Gran Sport. Later, it was called California Gran Sport or Skylark Gran Sport. If a car had the Gran Sport label, the letters "GS" appeared on the back bumper.

The fastest Gran Sport had a large V-8 engine. It could complete a quarter-mile (0.4 km) in 16.6 seconds at a speed of 86 miles (138 km) per hour.

1970 Gran Sport 455

QUICK STATS

- **Years Built**: 1965 to 1975
- **Maximum Hp**: 350 hp (1970)
- **0 to 60 mph (97 kmh)**: 6 seconds

A Gran Sport burns out at a drag racing event.

In 1970, Buick came out with a faster model of the Gran Sport, the Stage 1 Gran Sport 455. Famous car magazine *Motor Trend* said this car was the fastest muscle car they had ever tested. In fact, many car experts say that the Stage 1 Gran Sport 455 is the fastest of all the GS cars. Its engine could make the car go from 0 to 60 miles per hour (97 kmh) in just 5.5 seconds.

FLEX YOUR KNOWLEDGE

Many muscle car fans like to read magazines such as *Car and Driver*, *Road & Track*, and *Hot Rod*. Experts from the magazines compare and drive cars to test speed, handling, and other features. They report their findings and write reviews in the magazines' articles.

BUICK

GRAND NATIONAL

The Buick Regal Grand National started in 1982 at the Daytona 500. It began as a special look for the regular Buick Regal car. This special look included a two-tone paint job with gray and black, a T-top roof with removable panels, a rear spoiler, a shifter in the middle of the front seats, bucket seats, and turbine-style alloy wheels.

However, it had a not-so-powerful 4.1-liter V-6 engine that only made 125 horsepower. Buick only made 215 of these cars. The 1982 Grand National is the rarest of all Buick Regal Grand National models.

QUICK STATS

- **Years Built**: 1982 to 1987
- **Maximum Hp**: 200 hp (1984)
- **0 to 60 mph (97 kmh)**: 7.5 seconds

A Grand National at the start of a race.

1987 Grand National

That same year, Buick also introduced the LeSabre Grand National, which is even more rare. Only 112 of these cars were made. Even though it had a front-wheel drive and a non-turbo four-cylinder engine, it had the same all-black color and blacked-out chrome trim as the other Buick Grand Nationals.

In 1984, Buick introduced a new Grand National. It was all black with very little chrome. Car experts praised it for its excellent performance. It had 200 horsepower and 300 pounds (136 kg) of twisting force under the hood. This rear-wheel-drive car could race through a quarter-mile (0.4 km) in just 15.9 seconds.

FLEX YOUR KNOWLEDGE

In 1984, Chevrolet launched a redesigned Corvette. It only had five more horsepower than the Buick Grand National. The Corvette was only eight-tenths of a second faster than the Buick in the quarter-mile (0.4 km). This made Buick and Chevy compete in horsepower. The rivalry lasted until 1987 when the powerful 1987 Buick Regal GNX became the last Grand National model.

SKYLARK

The Skylark was first made in 1953. It was a special convertible car for Buick's 50th birthday. It had unique wheels and body lines. Because it was a special car built to celebrate the company's anniversary, only a small number—1,690—were made that first year.

In 1970, Buick launched the Skylark GSX. The car wasn't initially planned for the 1970 model year. However, when it was introduced to the public at the Chicago Motor Show in February 1970, people loved it. Buick rushed to produce it, but due to the tight production schedule, only 678 cars were made.

FLEX YOUR KNOWLEDGE

The rushed 1970 Skylark GSX was offered in only two colors, Apollo White and Saturn Yellow. Apollo White is the rarest, with only 187 made. A few more, 491 units, were available in Saturn Yellow.

QUICK STATS

- **Years Built**: 1953 to 1954; 1961 to 1972; 1975 to 1998
- **Maximum Hp**: 350 hp (1970)
- **0 to 60 mph (97 kmh)**: under 6 seconds

Skylark GSX

    In 1971, Buick made improvements to the Skylark by putting in a new and bigger 455-cubic-inch (7.5 l) engine. In addition, some parts, including valves, the distributor, and the carburetor, were updated. The engine was made to work with different transmissions—3-speed or 4-speed—so buyers had more choice. Many experts say that the 1971 Skylark GSX was the best muscle car ever made by Buick.

CHEVROLET

Chevrolet has been making cars for more than a hundred years. William Durant and Louis Chevrolet founded the company in 1911. It became part of General Motors in 1918.

Chevrolet's journey into making powerful muscle cars began in the 1950s when there was a growing demand for fast, high-performance vehicles. Even though they were known for making family cars, Chevrolet decided to add some speed and power to their lineup.

In 1955, they introduced the Chevrolet Bel Air, which had a new small-block V-8 engine. This was a big step toward their future success in the world of muscle cars.

QUICK STATS
- **Company Headquarters**: Detroit, Michigan
- **Years of Operation**: 1911 to present
- **Best-Selling Muscle Car**: Camaro

Louis Chevrolet

FUN FACT
Louis Chevrolet (1878–1941) designed a race car called the Monroe. His brother Gaston Chevrolet drove it to victory in the 1920 Indianapolis 500.

Chevrolet played an important role during the Golden Age of Muscle Cars. In 1961, they introduced the Impala Super Sport. It had a V-8 engine and a sporty look. It quickly became popular.

In 1964, Chevrolet launched the Chevelle SS, which was a medium-sized muscle car with a lot of power. The Camaro, Corvette Stingray, Nova, and El Camino soon followed, giving Chevrolet a strong collection of muscle cars.

Today, Chevrolet continues to make muscle cars. The Chevrolet Camaro is offered in different versions, such as SS and ZL1. The newer Corvette C8 has become an example of modern muscle car engineering.

1974 Corvette Stingray

CHEVROLET

BEL AIR

In 1950, Chevrolet launched the first generation of Bel Air, called Styleline Deluxe. The Chevrolet Bel Air was part of Chevrolet's full-size car lineup. It was a popular choice for drivers looking for a comfortable and stylish family car, but it was not yet a muscle car.

In 1961, Chevrolet came out with a new version of the Bel Air, with a powerful 409-cubic-inch (6.7 l) V-8 engine. This model was fast and lightweight. It became famous for hitting top speeds in drag races.

FUN FACT

The Beach Boys song "409" is about driving a car with a Chevrolet 409 engine.

1957 Bel Air

1963 Bel Air

The Chevrolet Bel Air included high-performance versions, such as the Bel Air Nomad, which had a more powerful engine and additional features to increase its performance. The Nomad also had large, curved rear side windows that people described as "bubble top" or "kitchen window."

The Super Sport debuted in 1961. This Bel Air model had a unique grille design, special emblems, and trim details.

One of the central features of the Bel Air SS was its powerful V-8 engine. The 1961 version was equipped with a 409-cubic-inch (6.7 l) V-8 engine, which, with the optional "Super Turbo-Thrust" package, could produce up to 360 or 409 horsepower.

QUICK STATS

- **Years Built**: 1950 to 1981
- **Maximum Hp**: 135 hp (1961)
- **0 to 60 mph (97 kmh)**: 8.7 seconds

CHEVROLET

NASCAR

The Bel Air SS received performance upgrades to match its high-power engine. These included a heavy-duty suspension, larger brakes, and dual exhausts, all of which added to its performance capabilities.

Chevrolet made even more changes to the Bel Air to make it more competitive in NASCAR. These included engine updates, suspension improvements, and other performance tweaks to meet the demands of the racing environment.

NASCAR's top division was called the Grand National Division, which later became the Winston Cup Series and eventually the Monster Energy NASCAR Cup Series.

A Bel Air races in Pomona, California.

Rex White

Many well-known drivers raced Chevrolet Bel Airs in NASCAR, including Rex White. White won the Grand National Championship (now known as the Cup Series) in 1960 driving a 1960 Chevrolet Bel Air. His championship win was a triumph for Chevrolet.

FLEX YOUR KNOWLEDGE

NASCAR stands for the National Association for Stock Car Auto Racing. It is one of the most popular types of auto racing. NASCAR races feature cars that look like regular, everyday cars. But under the hood, they have strong engines and special modifications to make them race ready. Muscle cars, like the Bel Air, were often driven in NASCAR races.

1960 Biscayne

BISCAYNE

Biscayne muscle car models were built from 1958 to 1975. Unlike other muscle cars, the Biscayne was considered to be fairly comfortable and roomy inside. It was ideal for long-distance cruising.

While the Biscayne was not primarily designed for racing, it found some use in motorsports during this era. It was a common choice for drag racing enthusiasts and amateur, or nonprofessional, racers due to its powerful engine options and solid build.

One notable example is the "427 Mystery Motor" Biscayne, which featured a potent 427-cubic-inch (7 l) V-8 engine designed for drag racing. This engine, coupled with the Biscayne's lightweight construction, made it a fierce competitor on the drag strips of the time.

The Biscayne was also occasionally used in NASCAR races, especially in the early years of this era when stock cars closely resembled the cars that were sold to the public. However, the Biscayne was typically overshadowed by other cars like the Chevrolet Impala, which were built for racing.

The 1968 Biscayne model is thought to be the fastest and most powerful. Its 425-cubic-inch (7 l) V-8 engine had 385 horsepower. It could hit the quarter-mile (0.4 km) mark in only 14.1 seconds.

QUICK STATS

- **Years Built**: 1958 to 1975
- **Maximum Hp**: 145 hp (1968)
- **0 to 60 mph (97 kmh)**: 6.1 seconds

FUN FACT

The Chevrolet Biscayne was used by police and taxi companies because it was dependable and inexpensive.

CHEVROLET

CAMARO

Chevrolet introduced the Camaro to directly compete with the Ford Mustang in the pony car market. Ford had great success with the Mustang. Chevrolet hoped the Camaro would offer a sporty, compact, and affordable alternative.

The Camaro and the Ford Mustang had an ongoing rivalry. Chevrolet kept the Camaro a secret project until its launch in 1966. They didn't want Ford or other carmakers to know about it. For many years, Chevrolet and Ford tried to outdo each other with faster and better cars.

The Camaro had a long hood, a low roofline, and a sleek shape. The interior was comfortable. And it came with options like racing stripes and spoilers.

QUICK STATS

- **Years Built**: 1967 to 2002; 2010 to 2024
- **Maximum Hp**: 360 hp (1970)
- **0 to 60 mph (97 kmh)**: 5.8 seconds

FLEX YOUR KNOWLEDGE

The Camaro's original name was Panther. A few weeks before it was released, Chevrolet changed the name to Camaro, which comes from the French word *camarade*, meaning "friend" or "pal."

In 1969, Chevrolet created the Camaro Z28. It was built for racing. It could go from 0 to 60 miles per hour (97 kmh) in only 7.4 seconds. Its quarter-mile (0.4 km) time was 14.8 seconds.

All-wheel disc brakes with special pistons were added to the 1969 Camaro SS. This helped the car drive better. As a result, the Camaro SS had many wins in NASCAR's Trans Am Series.

By 1970, the Camaro had even more powerful engines. The fastest was the 1970 Chevrolet Camaro with the Z28 package. This car could go from 0 to 60 miles per hour (97 kmh) in 5.8 seconds, and it could finish a quarter-mile (0.4 km) race in 14.2 seconds.

1970 Camaro RS

CHEVROLET

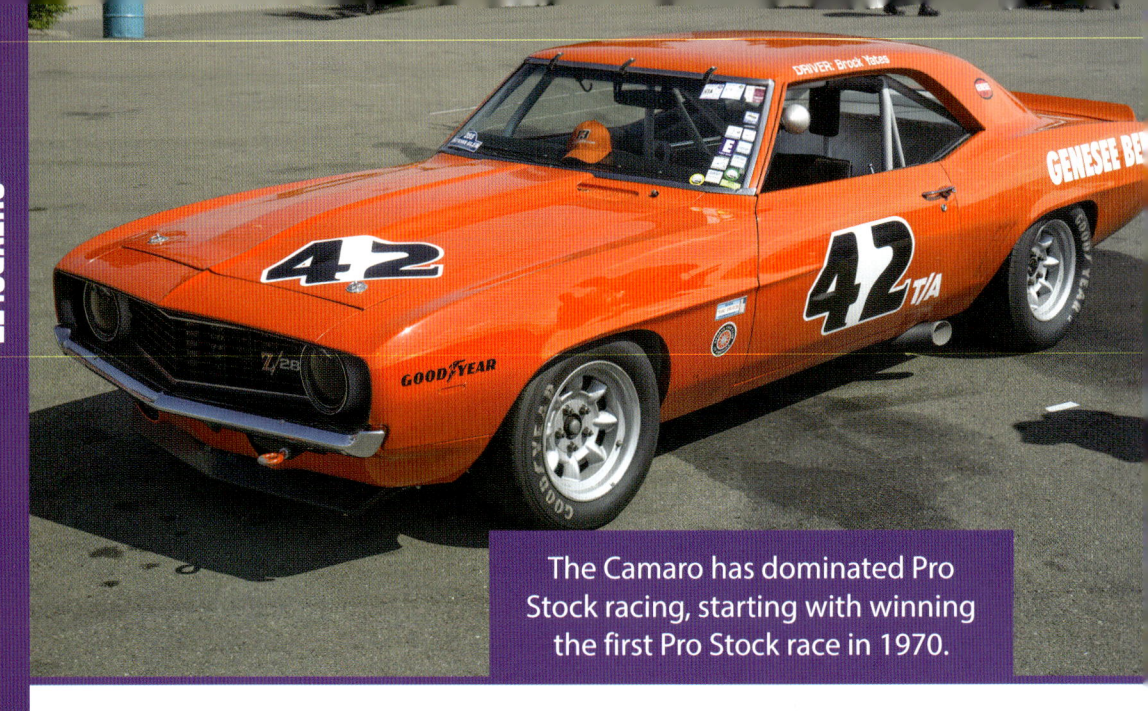

The Camaro has dominated Pro Stock racing, starting with winning the first Pro Stock race in 1970.

The Camaro was a favorite in the world of motorsports. It raced in events like the Trans-Am Series and in Pro Stock races, where it showed off its speed and handling. Drivers like Mark Donohue, who drove a Camaro for Roger Penske's team, made the Camaro a force to be reckoned with in Trans-Am competitions.

The Camaro also participated in drag racing events, achieving many victories in various competitions.

FLEX YOUR KNOWLEDGE

Pro Stock racing gives fans the chance to see what cars are like right off the showroom floor. These races feature cars that are only slightly modified from their street versions. Pro Stock racing is all about how well drivers handle their cars.

The Camaro's iconic status extends beyond the racetrack. It has been in many movies and television shows. It was one of the cars featured in the *Fast & Furious* movies. One of its most famous appearances was in the *Transformers* movies. The character Bumblebee is a 1977 Camaro that transforms into a robot.

During the 1970s, new government rules made carmakers focus on reducing emissions and making cars more fuel efficient. This meant smaller engines and less horsepower. The Camaro had to adapt, and, as a result, its driving performance wasn't as strong as it had been in previous years.

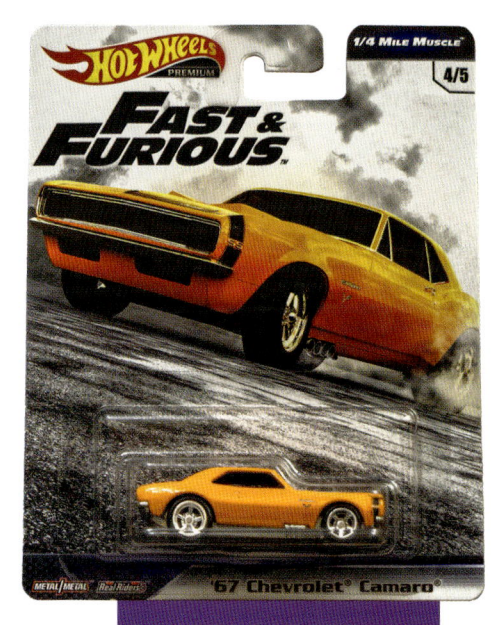

Many toy Camaros have been made over the years, including a Hot Wheels car.

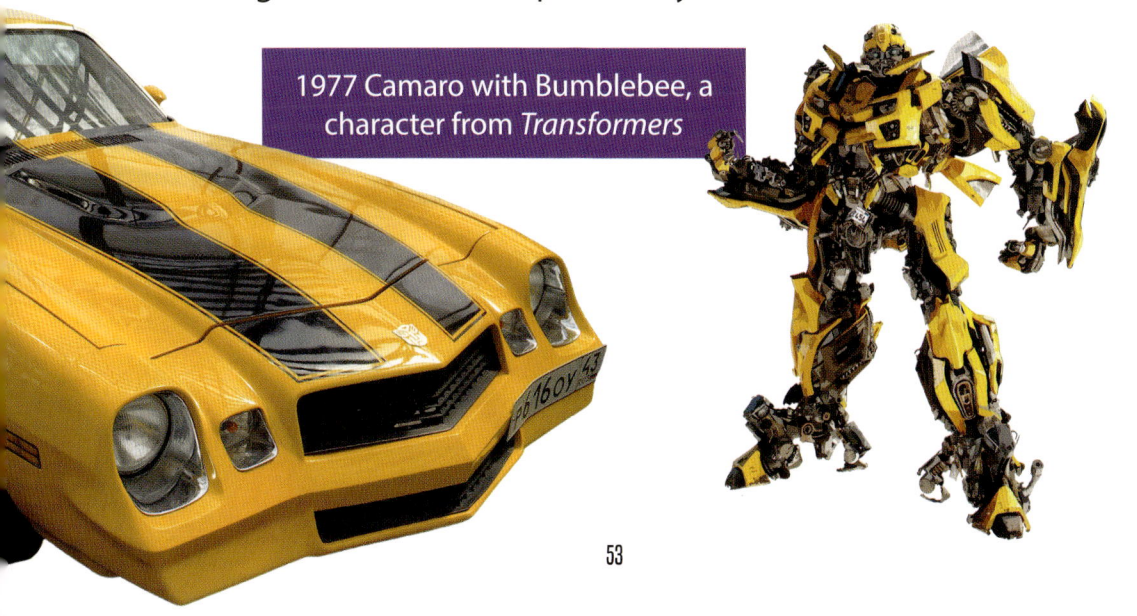

1977 Camaro with Bumblebee, a character from *Transformers*

CHEVROLET

CHEVELLE

Chevrolet designed the Chevelle to compete with the Ford Fairlane. The Chevelle was built on the A-body platform, which was the same one used for cars like the Pontiac Tempest, Buick Skylark, and Oldsmobile Cutlass.

Around mid-1964, Chevrolet replaced the top engine in the Chevelle with a more powerful 327 cubic inches (5.4 l) that produced 300 horsepower. GM wanted the Chevelle to be a strong competitor in the fast-growing performance car category.

QUICK STATS

- **Years Built**: 1964 to 1977
- **Maximum Hp**: 450 hp (1970)
- **0 to 60 mph (97 kmh)**: 6.1 seconds

By the time the 1965 models were released, Chevrolet made the Chevelle even more powerful. They introduced a 350-horsepower L79 engine for the Super Sport (SS) model. This was an important move. The 350-horsepower engine marked the beginning of the muscle car era, known for powerful and fast cars. However, in 1965, only 201 SS Chevelles were made, which disappointed many excited fans.

The 1970 Chevrolet Chevelle SS 454 was nicknamed "The King of the Streets" because it had the largest and most powerful engine of the year. The 454 engine was the biggest engine ever placed in a non-racing car up to and through 1970. This model is popular in movies and on television. It appears in shows such as *Supernatural*, *Wild America*, *Hawaii Five-O*, and *NCIS*.

1970 Chevelle SS

FUN FACT

In 2013, a vintage Chevelle SS 454 LS6 was sold for $1.15 million.

CHEVROLET

CORVETTE

In 1953, the Corvette made its debut at the GM Motorama show in New York City. At first, Chevrolet struggled to find buyers for the new Corvette. It produced only 300 Corvettes that first year.

In 1961, Chevrolet gave the Corvette a new look. The updated Corvette had four taillights. These became a famous feature of the car. The next year, in 1962, Chevrolet put a 330-cubic-inch (5.4 l) V-8 engine into the Corvette. The Corvette was becoming a muscle car.

1962 Corvette

FUN FACT
The Corvette was named after a small warship.

QUICK STATS
- **Years Built**: 1953 to present
- **Maximum Hp**: 360 hp (1962)
- **0 to 60 mph (97 kmh)**: 5.9 seconds

1965 Corvette Stingray

In 1963, the Corvette went through a big change. It had a new coupe body style with a fixed roof instead of a convertible type. The two-door car had a unique split-window design at the back. It became known as the Stingray.

By 1965, Chevrolet had added a big-block V-8 engine to the Corvette. This engine had a size of 396 cubic-inches (6.5 l) and was officially rated at 425 horsepower. This made the Stingray a racing powerhouse.

FLEX YOUR KNOWLEDGE

Corvettes, beginning with the first model in 1953, had fiberglass bodies. They were one of the first cars to be made with this lighter-weight material.

CHEVROLET

    Through the 1960s, Chevrolet continued to upgrade the Corvette's engine to make it bigger and more powerful. The Corvette's power on the racetrack made it famous. It appeared in several television shows from the 1960s and 1970s, including *Route 66* and *The Rockford Files*, and it had a movie named after it. *Corvette Summer* appeared in movie theaters in 1978.

    Chevrolet continued to make changes to the Corvette. The car became safer with the addition of features such as warning lights. In the 1970s, a new grille and broad bumpers were added. By 1977, Chevrolet had made 500,000 Corvettes.

1960 Corvette

In 1978, the Corvette got an updated look. It had a sleek, fastback shape. A special version of the car was made to honor the Indianapolis 500. Chevrolet has a long history with this famous race.

FLEX YOUR KNOWLEDGE

The Corvette has been the pace car at the Indianapolis 500 more than any other car. A pace car sets the speed for race cars to follow during the initial laps when tires and engines are warming up. In the case of an accident or bad weather, the pace car comes out, and the race cars follow it at a slower speed until the situation is cleared. Once everything is safe, the pace car leaves the track and the race resumes at full speed.

A Corvette pace car at the Indianapolis 500

CHEVROLET

EL CAMINO

The first El Camino came out in 1959. It had an unusual design. It had a cab like a regular car with a bed of a pickup truck. It was built to compete with the successful Ford Ranchero, which had been introduced in 1957. Not only was the design of the El Camino inspired by the Ranchero, but so was its name. Like Ford, Chevrolet chose a Spanish name for its new vehicle. *Ranchero* means "rancher" in Spanish. *El Camino* means "the way."

In 1960, Chevrolet brought out the second model of the El Camino. The car had new trim details that weren't popular. The car's price also went up. It was more expensive than the Ranchero. The 1960 El Camino didn't sell well. Chevrolet stopped making it for several years.

FUN FACT

The El Camino and the Ford Ranchero were based on Australian "utes," short for utility coupes, which had been popular with farmers since the 1930s.

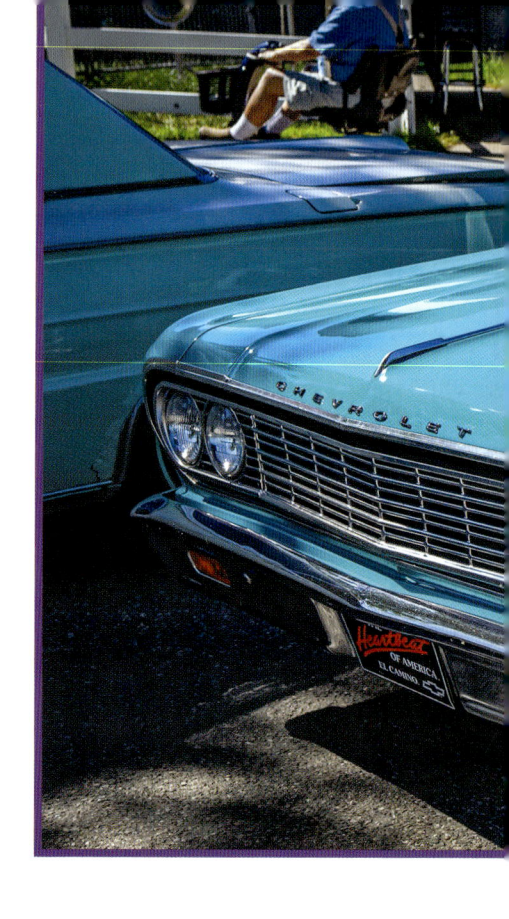

QUICK STATS

- **Years Built**: 1959 to 1960; 1964 to 1987
- **Maximum Hp**: 450 hp (1970)
- **0 to 60 mph (97 kmh)**: 5.2 seconds

1964 El Camino

In 1964, Chevrolet brought back the El Camino with a new design. People liked the look of the car. At first, it could make up to 155 horsepower. Later, it was given a V-8 engine that had 195 horsepower.

Over the years, Chevrolet continued to make modifications to the El Camino, which was quickly becoming a popular muscle car. The fastest El Camino in 1970 had 450 horsepower. The car was luxurious enough for passengers, but it was also powerful enough to go fast.

FLEX YOUR KNOWLEDGE

Some El Camino models had a "smuggler's box." It was a secret storage compartment hidden behind the front seat. It could be accessed through the truck bed.

CHEVROLET

IMPALA

The Impala made its debut in 1958. This first version was built to be a smaller version of the Bel Air. It had round headlights and two sets of three taillights, which was a unique feature for Chevrolet cars during this time. It wasn't until the 1963 model, though, that truly marked the entry of the Impala into the muscle car market. This 1963 Impala was a two-door coupe. It was smaller than previous models. Many thought it had the best of both worlds: comfort and speed.

To celebrate the production of the 50 millionth Chevrolet in 1963, the carmaker built a shiny gold-colored Impala. These Impalas were easy to identify not only because of their gold color but also because they were wider than other cars. The 1963 model had a 409 V-8 engine, which made 409 horsepower.

The Impala was named after an antelope that lives in Africa.

Later, there were newer versions of the Impala, like the SS 427, which had even stronger engines that could go fast. The Impala SS 427 had wide tires and extras like racing stripes and hood scoops that made it stand out.

In 1965 and 1966, the most popular car in the country was the Impala. It sold more than a million cars in both those years, making it the car that sold the most in a single year in the history of the United States.

QUICK STATS

- **Years Built**: 1957 to 1985; 1994 to 1996; 1999 to 2020
- **Maximum Hp**: 425 hp (1963)
- **0 to 60 mph (97 kmh)**: 6.3 seconds

1964 Impala

CHEVROLET

The Impala has become a classic among muscle car fans. Restoring old Impalas and adding modifications such as a hydraulic system, have become big businesses in the car industry.

Over the years, the Impala has been in many television shows, music videos, and movies, such as *American Graffiti*, *Goodfellas*, and *Boyz in the Hood*. In addition, the Impala has had a presence in law enforcement. Thanks to the car's durability and spacious interior, it has served as both a police car and as a taxicab.

The Impala was made for many years—over four decades from 1958 to 1996. It was briefly discontinued but returned in 2000. It has seen various design changes over the years, from the sleek, round head and taillights of the 1958 model to the boxier designs of the 1970s and 1980s.

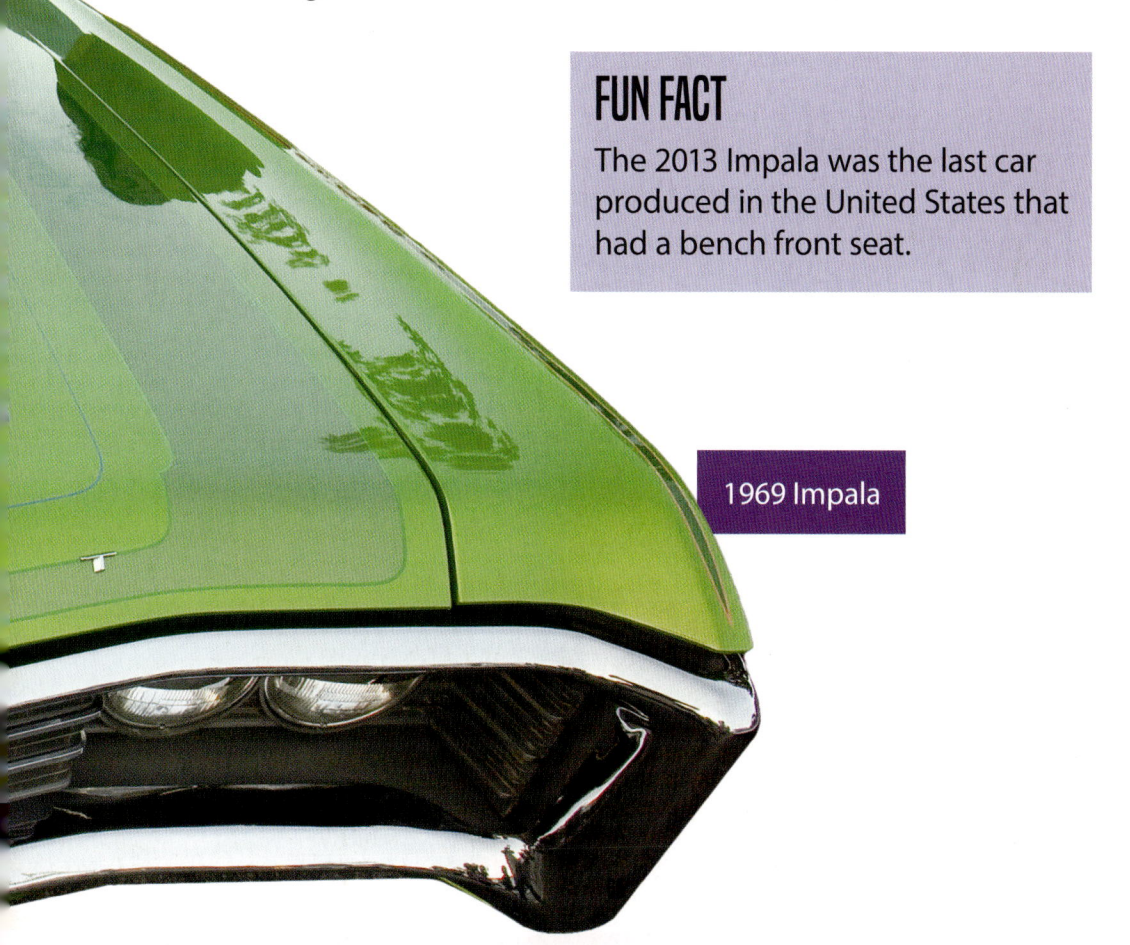

FUN FACT
The 2013 Impala was the last car produced in the United States that had a bench front seat.

1969 Impala

CHEVROLET

MALIBU

In 1964, Chevrolet introduced the Malibu. It was based on the Chevelle. The Malibu was available as a hardtop or a convertible.

In 1965, Chevrolet made changes to make the Malibu look sleeker. The car became a fastback. The fresh new look became popular. A sportier version called the Malibu SS was also offered as an option.

1964 Malibu

FUN FACT

From 1973 to 1983, the Malibu was the car Chevrolet raced in NASCAR.

QUICK STATS

- **Years Built**: 1964 to 1983; 1997 to present
- **Maximum Hp**: 450 hp (1970)
- **0 to 60 mph (97 kmh)**: 6.5 seconds

The 1970 Malibu SS 454 is thought to be the fastest and most powerful Malibu model. It had a 454-cubic-inch (7.4 l) V-8 engine that could produce around 450 horsepower. It also was a little roomier inside than previous models.

In the late 1970s, people wanted cars that used less gas. The Malibu became smaller to save fuel. By the mid-1970s, the model's muscle car years ended. Chevrolet still makes cars with the Malibu name, but beginning in 1978, the Malibu became a more fuel-efficient, family-sized car.

> **FLEX YOUR KNOWLEDGE**
>
> Torque is the rotational force produced by the engine. The greater the torque, the faster the car's wheels can turn. Powerful torque helps a car accelerate quickly and maintain speed on hilly roads. The 1970 Malibu SS 454 had 500 pounds per feet (978 Newton-meters) of torque. It could hit and maintain speeds of 130 to 140 miles per hour (209 to 225 kmh).

1970 Malibu SS

CHEVROLET

MONTE CARLO

The Monte Carlo was introduced in 1969 and went on sale in 1970. It was named after a city in Monaco that's known for its luxury. The Monte Carlo had a sleek and elegant body style. It was a two-door coupe with a long hood and a shorter rear deck. Its wheel arches were slightly flared to allow for wider wheels and tires. Some models featured a functional hood scoop.

FLEX YOUR KNOWLEDGE

Famous NASCAR drivers Jeff Gordon, Dale Earnhardt Sr., and Dale Earnhardt Jr. have all driven Monte Carlos.

Dale Earnhardt Sr. races a Monte Carlo at the Darlington Speedway.

1971 Monte Carlo

QUICK STATS

- **Years Built**: 1970 to 1988; 1995 to 2007
- **Maximum Hp**: 360 hp (1970)
- **0 to 60 mph (97 kmh)**: 8 to 14 seconds

Ever since NASCAR started its first races in 1949, there have been 16 different car companies that have won races. But Chevrolet has had the most wins. And the Monte Carlo has helped the car company achieve them. Across all of its generations, the Monte Carlo has the most wins of any car in the NASCAR Cup series. But the car's most successful years were from 1973 to 1977. It's no surprise, then, that 1973 and 1974 were strong sales years for the car.

In the early 2000s, Chevrolet built several special Monte Carlo versions to celebrate some of its racing stars, such as Dale Earnhardt Sr.

As of 2022, Chevrolet was still leading NASCAR with 814 race wins, 33 drivers winning championships, and 40 Manufacturers' Championships.

CHEVROLET

1964 Nova

NOVA

The Chevrolet Nova was introduced in 1962, but it wasn't until the 1964 model that it was considered a true muscle car.

In 1964, the most powerful engine available in the Chevrolet Nova SS was the 283-cubic-inch (4.6 l) Turbo-Fire V-8 engine. It was the first year the Nova was offered with a V-8 engine. "SS" stands for Super Sport. SS models have higher-end finishes, engines, and details.

QUICK STATS

- **Years Built**: 1962 to 1979; 1985 to 1988
- **Maximum Hp**: 195 hp (1964)
- **0 to 60 mph (97 kmh)**: 8.5 seconds

FUN FACT

In Spanish, *no va* means "doesn't go." Some people incorrectly say the Nova didn't sell well in Spanish-speaking countries because of its name. But the Nova was a popular car everywhere it was sold.

The 1968 Nova SS came with a V-8 engine that produced 295 horsepower. But buyers could upgrade the engine to a V-8 that produced 359 horsepower or another V-8 that produced 375 horsepower.

From 1971 to 1972, Chevrolet built a special model of the Nova, called the Rally Nova, which was inspired by rally racing. Novas have competed in rally racing, but the Rally Nova was not built to race.

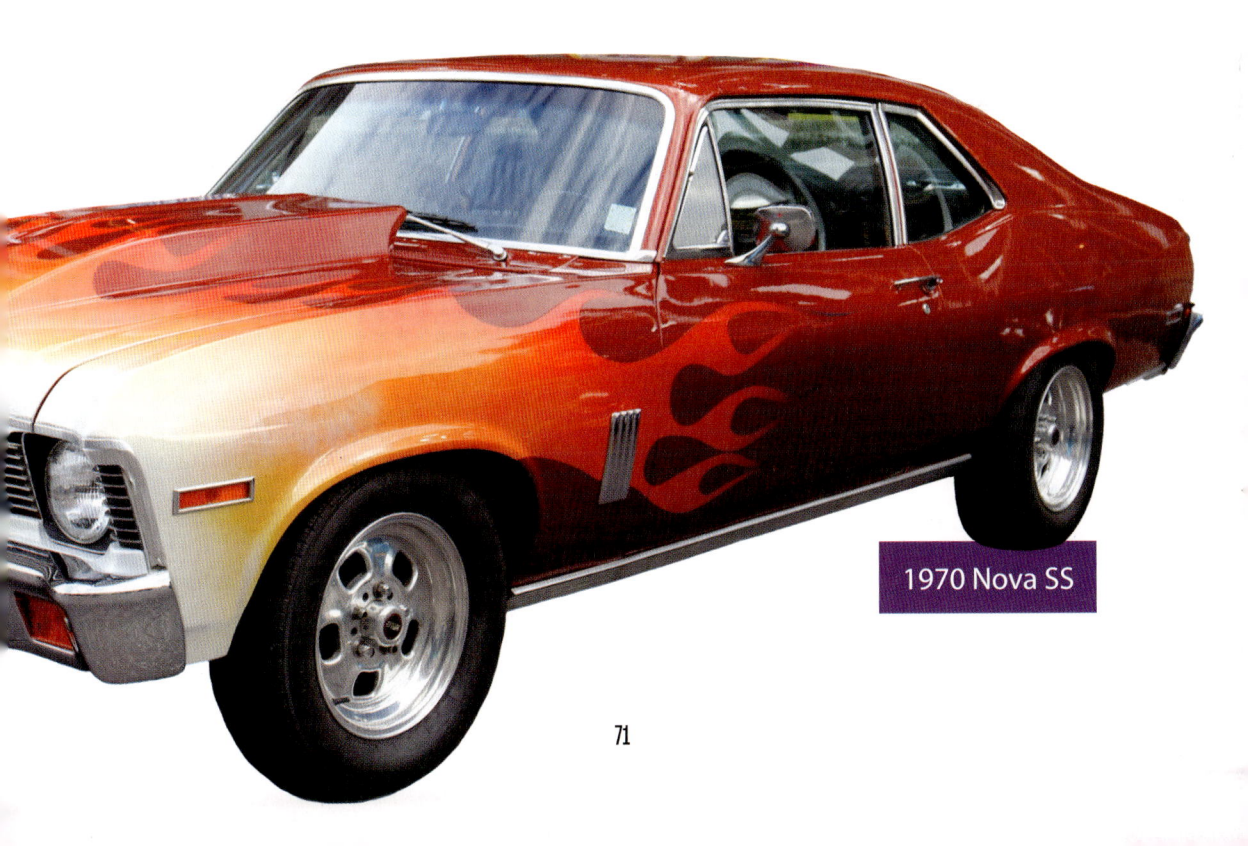

FLEX YOUR KNOWLEDGE

Rallying is a type of racing that takes place on dirt roads. Usually, competitors are not allowed to practice the route before the race. A passenger rides along with the driver. This person helps navigate the course.

1970 Nova SS

DODGE

Dodge has been making cars for more than 100 years. The company was started in 1900 by brothers Horace and John Dodge. They began by making parts for cars.

In 1914, they made their first complete car, the Model 30. People liked it because it was durable and not too expensive.

During World War I, Dodge built trucks and ambulances for the army. By the 1920s, Dodge was well-known. In 1928, Dodge was bought by the Chrysler Corporation, becoming part of a large company of cars.

QUICK STATS
- **Company Headquarters**: Auburn Hills, Michigan
- **Years of Operation**: 1900 to present
- **Best-Selling Muscle Car**: Challenger

1969 Charger

2017 Hellcat

Dodge made all sorts of vehicles over time, like cars, trucks, and muscle cars. The late 1960s and early 1970s were special decades for Dodge, thanks to their famous muscle cars.

The 1966 Dodge Charger became a popular car. In 1969, Dodge introduced another famous car, the Dodge Challenger. It had powerful engine options and a tough look. The Challenger became a strong competitor in the muscle car world and is still made and loved by car enthusiasts today.

Today, Dodge is known for fast cars like the Hellcat and Demon. These cars have strong engines like classic muscle cars once did.

FUN FACT

Before making parts for cars, the Dodge brothers built bicycles and parts for stoves.

CHALLENGER

Based on the Plymouth Barracuda, the first Dodge Challenger was built in 1969. The car was somewhat late to the muscle car scene, but it found immediate success. The Challenger had a variety of engine options. The fastest one had a powerful engine called the 426 Hemi V-8.

The early Dodge Challenger came in a two-door design. It was available in many different colors, and some had racing stripes on the sides. Since it was small, it was also known as a pony car.

QUICK STATS

- **Years Built**: 1969 to 1974; 1978 to 1983; 2008 to present
- **Maximum Hp**: 375 hp (1970)
- **0 to 60 mph (97 kmh)**: 5.8 seconds

1970 Challenger

Hemi V-8 engine

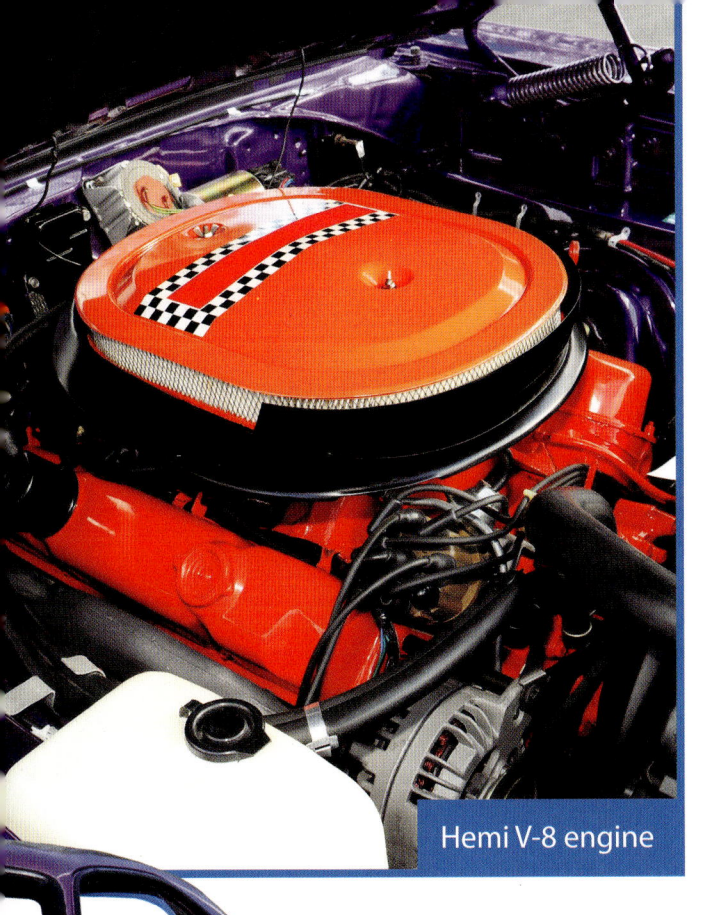

FLEX YOUR KNOWLEDGE

The Challenger was one of the first cars to have a Hemi engine. Hemis have round-shaped combustion chambers that look like half-spheres. This special design helps the engine retain heat, which makes it go faster.

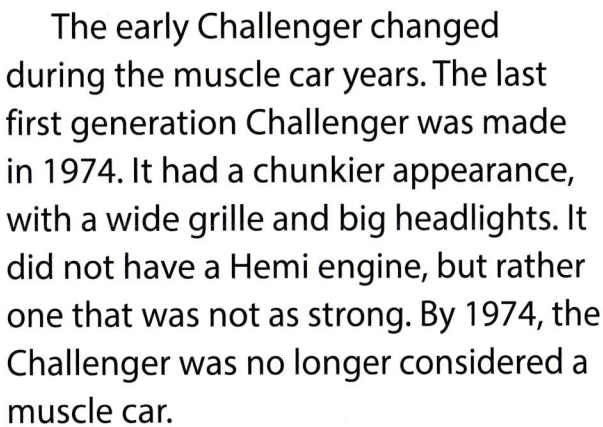

The early Challenger changed during the muscle car years. The last first generation Challenger was made in 1974. It had a chunkier appearance, with a wide grille and big headlights. It did not have a Hemi engine, but rather one that was not as strong. By 1974, the Challenger was no longer considered a muscle car.

In 2006, Dodge brought back the muscle car version of the Challenger. With a powerful engine and a retro design, it was a big hit.

DODGE

CHARGER

The Charger was introduced in 1966 to compete with other muscle cars such as the Ford Mustang and Chevrolet Camaro. The Charger quickly gained popularity and became an iconic muscle car of the era. It went through various design changes and generations over the years.

The 1968 to 1970 Charger, known as the second generation, is one of the most famous and recognized designs, featuring a coke-bottle shape and hidden headlamps. When the headlamps were not being used, they closed behind the front grille.

The 1969 Charger had a powerful 426 Hemi V-8 engine. Thanks to this upgrade, the Charger could go from 0 to 60 miles (97 km) per hour in six seconds. The car quickly became a star on the drag racing strips.

QUICK STATS

- **Years Built**: 1966 to 1978; 1981 to 1987; 2006 to present
- **Maximum Hp**: 425 hp (1966)
- **0 to 60 mph (97 kmh)**: 6.4 seconds

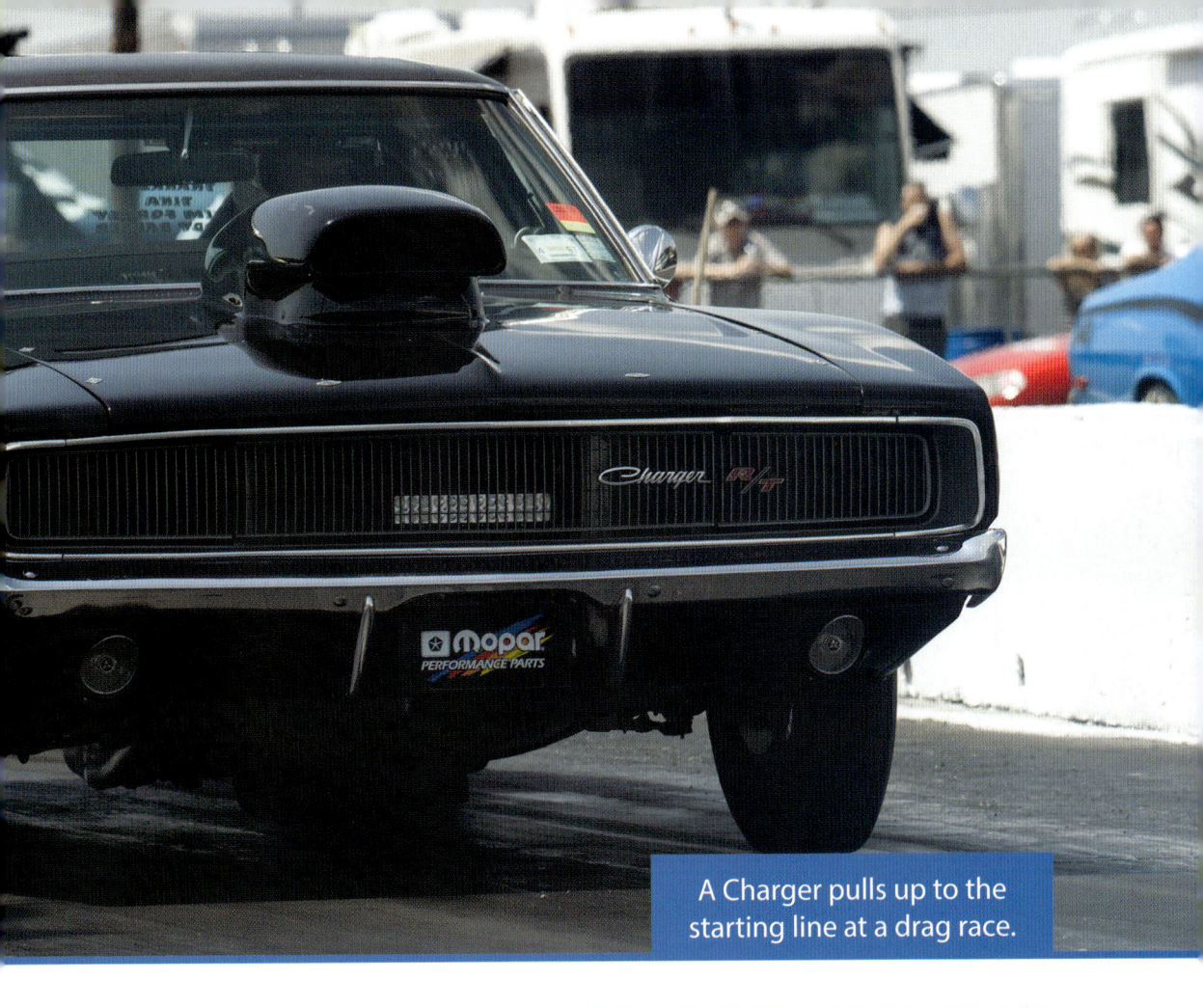

A Charger pulls up to the starting line at a drag race.

FLEX YOUR KNOWLEDGE

Drag racing takes place on a straight track as cars race for a quarter-mile (0.4 km). Muscle cars did not have great handling, but they had very fast acceleration. They quickly became popular in drag racing. Until the National Hot Rod Association was formed in 1951, drag racing was mostly an underground race. Now, there are drag racing strips all over the US.

DODGE

The Charger has been available in a variety of models, including the base model, high-performance models, and special editions such as the Charger Daytona, introduced in 1969, and the Charger Hellcat, introduced in 2015. It has also been offered with various engine options, ranging from V-6 engines to powerful V-8 Hemi engines, with some models producing over 700 horsepower.

Modern versions of the Charger have more advanced technology features such as touchscreen infotainment systems,

1960s Charger

2015 Charger Hellcat

driver assistance systems, and performance-enhancing technologies. The Charger remains a popular car for law enforcement. Chargers used by the police have special features and equipment.

The Dodge Charger is known for its performance, acceleration, and speed. Some of the high performance, modern-day versions can go from 0 to 60 miles per hour (97 kmh) in under four seconds and can reach top speeds of over 200 miles per hour (322 kmh). The Dodge Charger continues to be popular in the American muscle car market.

FUN FACT

A Dodge Charger called the General Lee from the television show *The Dukes of Hazzard* helped make the car popular. The Charger was later featured in the *Fast & Furious* movies.

General Lee

79

CHARGER DAYTONA

In the late 1960s, Chrysler and Ford competed to build the fastest cars for NASCAR. Both companies focused their designs on improving their cars' aerodynamics.

Both Chrysler and Ford created special cars to win races. Chrysler built the Dodge Charger Daytona in 1969. The Daytona had a unique design with a pointy front, a special grille, and a sloped back window. It also had a wing on the back that helped it grip the road. This aerodynamic design helped the car slice through the air as it raced around the track.

FUN FACT
Only 503 Dodge Charger Daytonas were built. Today, these rare cars are highly sought after by collectors.

QUICK STATS
- **Years Built**: 1969 to 1970; 2006 to 2009; 2013; 2017 to present
- **Maximum Hp**: 425 hp (1969)
- **0 to 60 mph (97 kmh)**: 5.2 seconds

Charger Daytona with Hemi 426

In 1970, the Dodge Charger Daytona, driven by Buddy Baker, was the first car to hit a top speed of more than 200 miles per hour (322 kmh) around a NASCAR track.

Ford came up with the Ford Torino Talladega to compete with the Dodge Charger Daytona. The competition between the Dodge Charger Daytona and the Ford Torino Talladega in the 1969 NASCAR season became known as the "Aero Wars."

The Aero Wars had a big impact on the regular car market. Many makers began designing cars with better aerodynamics and performance. The racing successes of cars like the Charger Daytona were important for the muscle car business. The idea was that if a car won on the racetrack, more people would want to buy that car from the dealership.

FLEX YOUR KNOWLEDGE

When the Charger Daytona first came out, many people thought the wing on the back was not good looking. The cars did not sell well. But their wings have made the car iconic. Today, these cars are worth a lot of money.

CORONET

The Dodge Coronet, especially its high performance models, had a powerful engine, making it competitive in racing.

The 426 Hemi-powered Coronet competed in the National Hot Rod Association (NHRA) drag racing events, including the Super Stock and Funny Car categories.

Funny Car

QUICK STATS
- **Years Built**: 1949 to 1959; 1965 to 1976
- **Maximum Hp**: 425 hp (1965)
- **0 to 60 mph (97 kmh)**: 5.3 seconds (1965)

FLEX YOUR KNOWLEDGE

Funny Car is a type of drag racing category. Funny cars have shorter wheelbases than street cars. They are made to look like regular cars, but they have bodies that pop up from the chassis. They got their name because when they first came out, someone thought they were "funny-looking" or a bit strange.

In the late 1960s and early 1970s, Coronet models like the R/T were used in NASCAR races. R/T stands for "Road and Track." That means the car can be used as a daily driver on the road but is also ready to race on a track. In 1969, the Dodge Coronet 500 won several NASCAR races. It helped Dodge become famous in the world of racing cars.

Muscle cars are known for being fast, but they are also known for being loud. In 1963, Dodge came up with the Torsion Quiet Ride. It was a layer of rubber that insulated the cabin. This not only kept it quieter inside, but it also made for a smoother ride.

1969 Coronet R/T

DODGE

DART

The Dodge Dart first came out in 1960 as a small car. It was made to be smaller and cheaper than other Dodge cars. At first, the Dart came in different styles, like sedans, convertibles, and wagons. People liked it because it was affordable and reliable.

From 1966 to 1969, Dodge offered the Dart GTS. This version was a true racing car. It had a powerful V-8 engine and a sleek, aerodynamic design. Car fans say that the 1969 Dart was the fastest and best muscle car model. It could hit a quarter-mile (0.4 km) stretch in 14 seconds.

FUN FACT
Dodge dealerships put large dartboards outside their showrooms to help advertise the Dart.

1970s Dodge Dart

In 1971, Dodge introduced the Demon, which was a higher-end model of the Dart. It was a little smaller and easier to handle on the road. But people thought the name sounded too evil. After a few years, Dodge changed the name to Dart Sport.

There have been several versions of the Dart. Many taxi companies in the 1960s and 1970s used Darts. In fact, Dodge made a version just for taxi drivers that included a yellow paint job. In 1974, the Hang Ten Dart was a model that came with a surfboard.

QUICK STATS

- **Years Built**: 1960 to 1976; 2013 to 2016
- **Maximum Hp**: 275 hp (1971)
- **0 to 60 mph (97 kmh)**: 7.8 seconds

DODGE

1969 Super Bee

SUPER BEE

The Dodge Super Bee, a limited-production muscle car, was produced from 1968 to 1971. It was based on the Dodge Coronet. It was built to compete with the Plymouth Road Runner, a low-priced muscle car.

The Super Bee came with features to give it better performance. These included a heavy-duty suspension, a four-speed manual transmission, and high-performance tires. The Super Bee also came with racing stripes that circled the tail of the car.

FUN FACT

Because Dodge and Plymouth were sister companies, the Road Runner and the Super Bee used the same chassis and the same engines.

QUICK STATS

- **Years Built:** 1968 to 1971
- **Maximum Hp:** 425 hp (1970)
- **0 to 60 mph (97 kmh):** 5.3 seconds

The front of the Super Bee had a special grille with two headlights on each side. Many Super Bee models had big hoods with two hood scoops. This not only made the car look tough but also helped the engine get more air.

In 1969, Dodge produced a Super Bee with a Hemi six pack. This was a more powerful and faster model. It came with a large hood scoop with "Six Pack" written on the engine. A Hemi six pack has six cylinders under the engine hood. The cylinders are arranged in two rows of three—like a six pack of soda.

The Super Bee had "Scat Pack" stripe graphics that went around the back end of the car and included a logo.

DODGE

In 1970, the Super Bee got a new look. It came in bright colors with unusual names: Plum Crazy, Sublime, and Go-Mango. But the biggest change in its appearance was to the grille. Dodge changed the front of the Super Bee to have a split grille. It was shaped with two ovals that flared out. Many people did not like this change. Sales of the Super Bee went down. The following year, Dodge reshaped and flattened the oval grille.

The grille on the 1970 Super Bee was called "Bumble Bee Wings."

88

The 1971 Super Bee had a new engine, a small 340ci V-8 with 300 horsepower. It wasn't as fast as the 1971 Hemi six pack Super Bee, but it was affordable, so more people bought it.

The 1971 Hemi Super Bee is the hardest model for collectors to find. Only 22 were built that year. But it is known as the best performing Super Bee.

FLEX YOUR KNOWLEDGE

In 2007, Dodge brought back the Super Bee name. The 2007 Charger Super Bee came in bright yellow and included stripes and a Super Bee decal.

1971 Super Bee

FORD

The Ford Motor Company was started by Henry Ford in 1903. The Model A was the first Ford car. In 1908, the famous Model T was introduced.

The Ford Company worked to make cars faster and cheaper. In 1913, Henry Ford was the first to install an assembly line to mass produce cars. On an assembly line, cars are put together quickly and efficiently. This made the Model T cost less, so more people could afford to buy one.

During World War II, Ford made military vehicles. After the war, the company started making cars again.

QUICK STATS
- **Company Headquarters:** Dearborn, Michigan
- **Years of Operation:** 1903 to present
- **Best-Selling Muscle Car:** Mustang

Henry Ford with a Model T

1964 Ford Mustang

In 1964, Ford introduced the Mustang. The Mustang is one of the most well-known muscle cars. It appealed to young adults who were looking for cars that were stylish, provided a sense of independence, and yet were also affordable. The Mustang's success spurred the production of muscle cars across the industry. Its speed and style continue to inspire car design.

In the 1960s, Ford also introduced the Torino and the Galaxie. Many considered them to look stylish. They were often used in races.

Ford has a long history of making affordable and appealing cars. They've made fast and smooth muscle cars, and they've also worked on making cars that are better for the environment. Today, they're still a large and important car company.

FORD

CAPRI

The first Ford Capri was made for drivers in Europe as a European version of the Ford Mustang. It came out in 1969, and by the next year, it was also available to drivers in the United States. The two-door coupe became very popular. It sold almost 1.9 million cars in the 17 years that it was made.

Initially, Ford wanted to call the Capri the "Colt" because it was like the little brother of the Mustang. But Mitsubishi, a car company from Japan, wanted to use the name for one of their cars. Ford was not able to use it. The car was called the Capri instead. It was named after a small Italian island.

1970s Capri

1975 Capri RS 3100

The Capri offered different engines, just like the Mustang. It started with smaller 1.3-liter and 1.6-liter engines that had 52 and 63 horsepower. Later, a 2.0-liter engine with 92 horsepower and a 3.0-liter engine with 136 horsepower were added as options.

In 1974, Ford entered a Capri into a racing championship called the European Touring Car Championship (ETCC). This led to the making of the fastest Capri, the RS 3100.

The RS 3100 had a 3.1-liter engine with 146 horsepower and a lot of torque. It also had special brakes, a lower and stiffer suspension, a sports exhaust, and a ducktail spoiler. The RS 3100, along with other Capri models, won numerous races.

QUICK STATS

- **Years Built**: 1968 to 1986
- **Maximum Hp**: 150 hp (1974)
- **0 to 60 mph (97 kmh)**: 7.3 seconds

FUN FACT

The Capri RS 3100 was only sold in the United Kingdom.

FORD

1968 Fairlane

FAIRLANE

The Ford Fairlane had been built since 1955, but in 1962, the Fairlane was redesigned. The body and frame of the 1962 Fairlane were made as one piece, which is called a unibody. Unibodies had been around for a while, but it wasn't until the late 1950s that carmakers began using unibodies in large numbers. The unibody included torque boxes, which help the car handle bumpy roads by moving slightly up and down. This made for a smoother ride.

Through the years, Ford kept making the Fairlane faster and better. Their styles changed frequently too. In the middle of 1963, Ford brought out a special version of the Fairlane called the Sports Coupe. It was sportier and had bucket seats and a small console on the floor.

QUICK STATS

- **Years Built**: 1955 to 1970
- **Maximum Hp**: 335 hp (1968)
- **0 to 60 mph (97 kmh)**: 5.5 seconds

In 1964, Ford introduced the Fairlane Thunderbolt. It was built for drag strip racing. It had special modifications, like a more powerful engine and lightweight materials. Other features, like carpeting, a radio, and sun visors, were taken out to make the vehicle lighter and faster.

In 1970, the Ford Fairlane 500 had an extra special engine called the 429 Cobra Jet. This engine had a lot of power. It could make the car go from 0 to 60 miles per hour (97 kmh) in just 6.5 seconds.

1964 Fairlane Thunderbolt

GALAXIE

In the early 1960s, the Ford Galaxie was a favorite among NASCAR drivers because of its sleek appearance and fast, powerful engine. It won many races and championships.

The Galaxie also competed in drag racing in the 1960s. But the car was heavy and not as speedy as Ford wanted. To improve the car's performance, Ford made modifications to some of the Galaxie models to make them lighter. These included fiberglass parts, aluminum bumpers, and other lightweight materials.

QUICK STATS

- **Years Built**: 1959 to 1974
- **Maximum Hp**: 345 hp (1966)
- **0 to 60 mph (97 kmh)**: 5.8 seconds

1965 Galaxie 500

1963 Galaxie

In 1963, Ford introduced a sports hardtop Galaxie model. It had a unique fastback roof. It became popular, outselling the traditional models with flat roofs.

The most powerful model of the Galaxie 500 came out in 1966. It sold well. One version, the Cammer 427, was built for NASCAR. It had a horsepower of 650 hp. It was dangerously powerful, so NASCAR banned it.

FLEX YOUR KNOWLEDGE

The Space Race was a Cold War-era competition between the United States and the Soviet Union. Each country tried to outdo the other by achieving new milestones in space exploration, such as landing the first person on the moon. Ford picked the name "Galaxie" to make people think of space and exploration. They wanted to show that their cars were all about reaching new heights in design.

FORD

GT40

In the early 1960s, Ford and Italian race carmaker Ferrari had a rivalry. They each wanted to have the best race car with the most wins. Ford built a special car called the GT40. It was small and sleek and had a powerful engine. The GT40 entered into a challenging car race in France called the 24 Hours of Le Mans.

Ford raced the car in the 24 Hours of Le Mans in 1964, but it had some problems and didn't do well. That same year, famous race car driver and car designer Carroll Shelby took over the Ford racing team. They worked on the GT40, making it faster and more reliable. In 1965, the GT40, driven by famous car driver Ken Miles, had its first win at NASCAR's Daytona 500.

QUICK STATS

- **Years Built**: 1964 to 1969
- **Maximum Hp**: 470 hp (1969)
- **0 to 60 mph (97 kmh)**: 4.7 seconds

The Ford team continued to make improvements to the GT40. One was a new type of brake changing system. By moving some brake parts around, the pit crew team could change a set of brakes a lot faster. The quick-change brakes meant less time in the pit and a faster return to the track.

In 1966, the GT40, driven by Bruce McLaren and Chris Amon, won its first 24 Hours of Le Mans race. The GT40 defeated Ferrari at Le Mans for four straight years.

Only 124 Ford GT40s were ever made. Original cars are rare and expensive, but there are many replicas, or copies, of the car today.

FUN FACT

The GT40 was named after its height. It was only 40 inches (102 cm) tall. The GT stands for "grand touring."

GT40

FORD

MUSTANG

The Ford Mustang's first generation, from 1965 to 1973, was the start of something special in the automotive industry.

In the 1960s, Ford wanted to make a car that would appeal to younger drivers. Before the Mustang was introduced, several different prototypes were shown to selected groups of young people. Ford gathered their feedback to use for the car's final design. The Mustang's design was also inspired by European cars, which were becoming more popular in the Unites States at that time.

FUN FACT
22,000 Mustangs were bought on the first day it went on sale.

QUICK STATS
- **Years Built**: 1964 to present
- **Maximum Hp**: 335 hp (1967)
- **0 to 60 mph (97 kmh)**: 7.1 seconds

1967 Mustang GTA

1969 Mustang

In 1964, Ford debuted the Ford Mustang at the New York World's Fair. It became a hit right away. Ford expected to sell about 100,000 Mustangs in the first year but ended up selling more than 400,000.

In 1968, the Mustang got a new two-spoke steering wheel. Ford also put turn signals on the front and back of the car.

The 1969 Ford Mustang 428 Cobra Jet was considered the fastest model. It came with a 428-cubic-inch (7 l) V-8 engine. And with a big engine comes big power—335 horsepower.

FLEX YOUR KNOWLEDGE

The 1964 Plymouth Barracuda was, technically, the first to be called a pony car, but the Mustang was the car that made the nickname famous.

FORD

1966 Mustang

Many people assume the Mustang was named after a horse. But that may not be the case. When designer John Najjar suggested calling the car a Mustang, he said the name came from a World War II fighter plane. The name was rejected. Later, Najjar pitched the idea again, saying the name came from the horse called a mustang. This time, the name was a hit and Ford adopted it.

The Mustang came in different styles: a coupe, a convertible, and a fastback. Although it offered many different colors, including blue, silver, white, black, green, brown, and yellow, red was the most popular.

FUN FACT
Red is still the most popular Mustang color today.

102

Since its debut in 1964, the Mustang has become an American icon. Many people connect the car to freedom and independence. Mustangs have been famous in pop culture, appearing in movies and television shows more than 3,300 times.

This famous Mustang grille emblem is known as Pony in Corral.

SHELBY MUSTANG

Race car driver Carroll Shelby helped design the first Ford Shelby Mustang. It was called the GT350, and it was considered a speed demon. It had a V-8 engine that could make more than 300 horsepower. It could hit the quarter-mile (0.4 km) mark in 13.6 seconds.

The GT350's suspension system allowed it to handle tight turns on a racetrack. People started calling the GT350 a "race car for the street." It was speedy, loud, and had racing stripes and badges.

QUICK STATS

- **Years Built**: 1965 to 1970; 2007 to present
- **Maximum Hp**: 306 hp (1965)
- **0 to 60 mph (97 kmh)**: 6.5 seconds

1965 Shelby GT350 Mustang

1967 Shelby Mustang GT500

In 1967, Ford introduced the Shelby Mustang GT500. It was like the GT350, but even more powerful. The GT500 had a V-8 engine that could make over 350 horsepower.

FUN FACT

The movie *Gone in 60 Seconds* features a 1967 Shelby Mustang GT500 named Eleanor.

The 1967 Shelby Mustang GT500 could accelerate from 0 to 60 miles per hour (97 kmh) in 6.2 seconds. It could hit the quarter-mile (0.4 km) mark in only 14.6 seconds. The car could also travel long distances and was considered comfortable inside. The 1967 GT500 had a new safety feature. It was the first production car to include a built-in rollover bar.

FORD

Carroll Shelby

While Shelby Mustangs were becoming famous on the streets, Carroll Shelby was also creating another legendary car, the Shelby Cobra. This car was small, lightweight, and had a big V-8 engine. It was made for racing and became a superstar on the racetrack.

It wasn't just the Cobra's wins in racing that made the car famous. Its design also helped it become iconic. The Cobra's popularity continues today. Car enthusiasts can buy a kit and build a replica of the Cobra themselves.

FLEX YOUR KNOWLEDGE

Carroll Shelby began his career as a chicken farmer but drove hot rods in drag races for fun. His interest in racing grew, but after discovering a heart problem, his racing career ended in 1960. Instead, he began building cars. The Cobra is one of his best-known creations.

Shelby wanted to produce the fastest car available for the road. He created the 1967 Shelby Cobra 427 Super Snake, turning a race car into a street-legal vehicle. The vehicle ran on the Cobra's 427-cubic-inch (7 l) V-8 engine. With the addition of a pair of superchargers, this vehicle went up to 800 horsepower. It had a top speed close to 200 miles per hour (322 kmh).

Despite this car's incredible power and performance, Shelby only built one of the Super Snakes. With so much power and speed, the car wasn't very practical for the road.

> **FUN FACT**
>
> In 2007, Ford brought back the Shelby Mustang with a new design. They are still being made today.

2007 Shelby Mustang GT500

FORD

THUNDERBIRD

The Thunderbird was introduced in 1955. Ford built it to compete with the Corvette. Car fans nicknamed the Thunderbird the "T-bird." The first-generation Thunderbird was a two-door coupe with a V-8 engine.

In 1958, the Thunderbird was redesigned. It became a larger, boxier, four-door sedan. Car fans called it the "Square Bird."

The third generation, known as the "Bullet Bird," was introduced in 1961. It had a sleek, bullet-like design and a bold front grille. These early Thunderbirds were powerful, but they were not muscle cars quite yet.

QUICK STATS

- **Years Built**: 1955 to 1997; 2002 to 2005
- **Maximum Hp**: 300 hp (1957)
- **0 to 60 mph (97 kmh)**: 8.5 seconds

1959 "Square Bird"

The fourth-generation Thunderbird, called the "Flair Bird," debuted in 1964. It featured a more angular and formal design. It didn't have the sleek lines of the Bullet Bird. This fourth-generation model could go from 0 to 60 miles per hour (97 kmh) in 8.9 seconds.

In 1967, the Thunderbird changed again. It became larger and more luxurious. It was available as a two-door coupe or four-door sedan.

1967 Thunderbird

FLEX YOUR KNOWLEDGE

Thunderbirds are often given nicknames by fans. The first models, built from 1955 to 1957, are sometimes called "Early Birds." Models built from 1972 to 1976 are called "Big Birds" because they are the biggest and heaviest models.

FORD

1967 Thunderbird

Like most carmakers in the 1970s, Ford changed its design of the Thunderbird to be more appealing to customers who were concerned about gas prices. The sixth generation of the Thunderbird was downsized. It was smaller and more fuel-efficient than its earlier models.

The seventh-generation Thunderbird, introduced in 1977, was a coupe that had luxury in mind. It featured more aerodynamic styling, and it was well-received by buyers. During this period, a T-top roof option was introduced, adding to the car's appeal.

FLEX YOUR KNOWLEDGE

In 1987, race car driver Bill Elliott set a NASCAR record for the fastest qualifying lap at the Talladega Superspeedway. He was driving a Thunderbird. He drove more than 212 miles per hour (341 kmh). Elliott still holds this record today.

Bill Elliott at Talladega Superspeedway

The 2002 Thunderbird was called the "Retro Bird" because of its vintage design.

The eleventh generation Thunderbird was introduced in 2002, marking the final production run of this iconic car.

It returned to its two-seat sports car roots, with a design similar to the original 1955 Thunderbird. It was available as a convertible with a removable hardtop. The 2002 model was known for its performance and style. Its retro look was appealing to buyers.

The Thunderbird has had its place in American pop culture. It's appeared in many movies and television shows. In 1986, country singer John Denver recorded a song about the Thunderbird called "Along for the Ride." The Beach Boys also sang a song about the Thunderbird called "Fun, Fun, Fun."

FUN FACT

From 1955 to 2005, more than 4.4 million Thunderbirds were built.

FORD

TORINO

The Ford Torino made its debut in 1968 as a mid-size car model. It was named after the city of Turin, Italy. It was built as a more upscale version of Ford's Fairlane. But it was also faster. It competed with Dodge Charger and the Chevrolet Chevelle.

In 1969, Ford made a special version of the Torino called the Torino Talladega. It was named for the Talladega Superspeedway, which opened the same year. The Torino Talladega had aerodynamics and was built for racing. This car was successful in NASCAR. Between 1969 and 1970, it had 29 wins.

QUICK STATS
- **Years Built**: 1968 to 1976
- **Maximum Hp**: 375 hp (1970)
- **0 to 60 mph (97 kmh)**: 6.7 seconds

Donnie Allison races a Torino Talladega in 1969.

1968 Torino GT

In 1970, Ford introduced the Torino GT and the high-performance Torino Cobra models. These came with powerful engines, including the 429 Cobra Jet. The Cobra Jet could make more than 375 horsepower.

Muscle cars, like the Torino GT and the Torino Talladega, were known to be gas guzzlers. Because they were built on larger and heavier frames than other cars, their engines had to work harder. And when engines work harder, they use more fuel.

At that time, many cars also had inefficient carburetors, which are like fuel mixers, and high compression ratios. This meant the engines burned more fuel to provide power.

FORD

As the 1970s progressed, the Ford Torino underwent changes to meet new rules about safety and pollution. In 1972, it took on a more formal, less sporty appearance. It was renamed the "Gran Torino."

The Gran Torino still offered the speed of a V-8 engine, but it became less of a muscle car and more of a luxury car.

The Gran Torino became famous after it was featured in the popular 1970s television show *Starsky & Hutch*.

114

1976 Gran Torino Elite

In 1974, Ford brought out the Torino Elite, which was a fancier version of the Gran Torino. This car had a unique and upscale look, and it was made for people who wanted a comfortable and stylish ride more than a fast one.

As time went on, the Torino changed and became a bigger car that focused on making the ride comfortable. The last year the Torino was made was 1976.

MERCURY

Mercury started in 1938 as a brand that was part of Ford. At first, Mercury made stylish cars with a bit more power, which appealed to buyers looking for a more upscale car than something basic.

Mercury made famous cars like the Mercury Eight and Mercury Monterey. These cars had V-8 engines, which made them powerful and popular.

In the 1960s, Mercury joined the muscle car trend. The carmaker made the Mercury Comet, a small car with V-8 engines for speed lovers. In 1967, they made the Cougar, a sporty car that was the Mercury version of the Ford Mustang.

FUN FACT
The Mercury brand was named after the Roman god of messengers, known for dependability and speed.

QUICK STATS
- **Company Headquarters**: Dearborn, Michigan
- **Years of Operation**: 1938 to 2011
- **Best-Selling Muscle Car**: Cougar

1956 Mercury Monterey

1970 Cougar Eliminator

The Cougar became famous and even had fast versions like the Cougar Eliminator. These Mercury muscle cars were exciting and looked cool. But in the 1970s, new rules made cars safer and use less fuel. Mercury, like others, had to change their cars.

Over time, Mercury made different models like the Grand Marquis. They also tried making SUVs and minivans. But in 2010, Ford stopped making Mercury cars due to a changing car market.

FLEX YOUR KNOWLEDGE

The Cougar was the best-selling Mercury of all time.

MERCURY

COMET

Mercury introduced the Comet in 1960 as a mid-sized car. It was based on the Ford Falcon and came in different styles, such as sedans, wagons, and convertibles. People liked the Comet for its simple design and reliable performance.

In the mid-1960s, the Mercury Comet became sportier. In 1964, the Comet Cyclone, with powerful V-8 engine options, was launched. This was to attract people who wanted fast cars. The Cyclone became known for its quick speed and good handling. It had a unique look with a special grille and bold stripes.

1966 Comet Cyclone

QUICK STATS
- **Years Built**: 1960 to 1969; 1971 to 1977
- **Maximum Hp**: 335 hp (1966)
- **0 to 60 mph (97 kmh)**: under 7 seconds

1976 Comet

In the early 1970s, the Mercury Comet became a smaller, compact car.

In its last years between 1974 and 1977, the Mercury Comet stayed practical and efficient. The Comet LN7 and Mercury Bobcat were introduced. These cars were dependable and focused on transportation over fancy features.

FLEX YOUR KNOWLEDGE

In 1963, Mercury wanted to show how dependable the Comet was. Three Comets were driven from Cape Horn at the tip of South America to Fairbanks, Alaska, in under 40 days. That's a trip of more than 16,000 miles (25,750 km).

MERCURY

COUGAR

The Cougar is the name used for a range of cars that were sold by Mercury. They were available from 1967 to 1997 and then from 1999 to 2002.

Two of the top Mercury Cougar muscle cars from 1967 to 1970 were the Eliminator and the XR-7 with high-performance options. Many car experts say that the Mercury Cougar Eliminator is the most famous muscle car in the Cougar family. The Eliminator package came out in 1969 and offered a choice of powerful V-8 engines, including the 428 Cobra Jet.

The Cougar Eliminator stood out with its unique style, bold graphics, and performance features such as a sturdy suspension, responsive steering, and a Ram Air system. The Eliminator was built to compete with other famous muscle cars of that time.

1967 Cougar XR7

1970 Cougar Eliminator

The regular Cougar XR-7 was known for its luxury and elegance. However, when buyers added high-performance options such as the 390 or 428 Cobra Jet engines, it transformed into a strong muscle car. The Cougar was very popular during the muscle car era, and it had many wins in drag racing.

QUICK STATS

- **Years Built**: 1967 to 1997; 1999 to 2002
- **Maximum Hp**: 335 hp (1969)
- **0 to 60 mph (97 kmh)**: 7.6 seconds

FUN FACT

Mercury first used a mountain lion as its logo, but it looked too similar to Jaguar's logo. The Mercury logo was changed, and "Cougar" was added underneath.

MERCURY

CYCLONE

In 1964, the Mercury Comet Cyclone burst onto the scene. Built on the compact Mercury Comet, the Cyclone merged power with style. It came in two-door hardtop and convertible models. It had a bold grille and side stripes.

In 1966, the Comet Cyclone GT debuted. It had several V-8 engine options, including the 390- and 427-cubic-inch (6.4 and 7 l). More buyers were interested in power, speed, and performance. This was Mercury's answer.

QUICK STATS

- **Years Built**: 1964 to 1971
- **Maximum Hp**: 335 hp (1968)
- **0 to 60 mph (97 kmh)**: 6.1 seconds

1969 Cyclone Cale Yarlborough Special

1969 Cyclone Cobra Jet

Mercury introduced the Cyclone 428 Cobra Jet in 1968. It could reach a quarter-mile (0.4 km) stretch in 13.86 seconds at top speeds of 101.6 miles per hour (164 kmh). Its sleek, fastback design was built for speed.

The Cyclone Spoiler II was built to compete in NASCAR. It won eight Grand National races between 1969 and 1970. People could purchase the Cyclone Spoiler. A special model was built in honor of famous NASCAR driver Cale Yarborough.

FUN FACT

Hot Wheels made a toy car based on the 1969 Mercury Cyclone.

MERCURY

1964 Maurader

MARAUDER

The Mercury Marauder's debut year is known as "1963 ½." This is because it was introduced during the middle of the 1963 model year. By offering a new car halfway through the year, Mercury didn't have to wait until the next full year to make changes to their line-up.

The fastest version of the Marauder with the most powerful V-8 engine could complete a quarter-mile (0.4 km) race in 15.6 seconds. In 1964, the Marauder had a lot of success in racing. It had five NASCAR wins.

QUICK STATS

- **Years Built**: 1963 to 1965; 1969 to 1970; 2003 to 2004
- **Maximum Hp**: 425 hp (1964)
- **0 to 60 mph (97 kmh)**: 7 seconds

In the 1950s and early 1960s, many Mercury cars had a unique roofline that included what was called the "Breezeway." The Breezeway was a roll-down or pop-up rear window that slanted inward. It allowed for more air, or ventilation, to come into the passenger cabin.

> **FUN FACT**
> A marauder is like a pirate, someone who moves from place to place making attacks and stealing from others. Mercury thought the tough name would be appealing to buyers.

Mercury changed its roofline for the Marauder. Its rear window slanted outward, more typical of other cars. This helped the Marauder's aerodynamics and, in turn, its success in NASCAR.

In 1969, the second-generation Marauder looked different. It was less boxy and had smooth, sleek lines. It came as a two-door or four-door car. With V-8 engines in sizes from 390 to 429 cubic inches (6.4 to 7 l), it was a powerful muscle car. A sportier version called the Marauder X-100 had special seats and a unique gear shifter.

1969 Marauder

OLDSMOBILE

Ransom E. Olds, an inventor and businessman, started the Olds Motor Works company in 1897. The company's name changed to Oldsmobile a few years later. In 1900, a fire destroyed all their cars except for one which had a special feature, a curved dash. A year later, Oldsmobile began selling the curved-dash car, and it became a hit.

The Curved Dash Oldsmobile was the first mass-produced vehicle.

Olds left the company in 1904, but Oldsmobile didn't do as well without him. It was bought by General Motors in 1908.

In 1939, Oldsmobile introduced the Hydra-Matic automatic transmission. Drivers didn't have to use a clutch to shift gears, which made driving easier. In 1949, Oldsmobile introduced the powerful Rocket V-8 engine into their cars.

QUICK STATS
- **Company Headquarters**: Lansing, Michigan
- **Years of Operation**: 1897 to 2004
- **Best-Selling Muscle Car**: 4-4-2

In the 1960s and 1970s, Oldsmobile entered the muscle car market. They introduced the 4-4-2 in 1964. Later, the Hurst and the Toronado would make their appearance on the market.

After the muscle car era, Oldsmobile kept making cars better. They were the first car company to put airbags in cars sold to the public. In 1980, they made a car with a diesel engine that used less gas, which is better for the environment.

Oldsmobile had many successful cars, including the Cutlass Supreme, which was the best-selling American car from 1976 to 1981 and again in 1983. But Oldsmobile sales went down in the 1990s. In 2004, Oldsmobile cars stopped being made.

FUN FACT

When Oldsmobile went out of business in 2004, it was the longest-running American carmaker. Over its 107 years, the company made more than 35 million vehicles.

1967 Cutlass

OLDSMOBILE

4-4-2

Oldsmobile introduced the 4-4-2 in 1964 to compete with the Pontiac GTO. Originally, the 4-4-2 was only a package that could be added to another Oldsmobile like the Cutlass. But in 1968, Oldsmobile made the 4-4-2 its own model.

The name "4-4-2" stood for three important things about the car's features. The first "4" referred to the car's engine that used a four-barrel carburetor, which made the car powerful and fast. The second "4" in the name meant that the car had a transmission with four speeds.

The "2" in the name was for the dual exhaust outlets. This is where the fumes and waste made by the car's engine go out. The dual outlets helped the car perform better. They also gave the car a sound like a growl.

1970 4-4-2

The 1968 4-4-2 was equipped with a ram air intake hose. This helped the car run more efficiently and have better gas mileage. It also gave the car more horsepower. When a car moves forward, air is forced into its system and into the engine. The engine needs the right mix of air and fuel to burn fuel effectively. A ram air system brings a steady flow of additional air into the engine. This can improve the air-fuel mix and helps the engine burn less fuel.

QUICK STATS

- **Years Built**: 1968 to 1971
- **Maximum Hp**: 350 hp (1968)
- **0 to 60 mph (97 kmh)**: 6.7 seconds

FLEX YOUR KNOWLEDGE

A lot of muscle cars, including the 4-4-2, had a shape that people called a "coke-bottle" design. These cars had a narrow body with taller fenders that surrounded it. The design reminded people of an old-fashioned Coca-Cola bottle.

OLDSMOBILE

HURST/OLDS

In 1968, a car product inventor named George Hurst decided to replace the engine in his Oldsmobile 4-4-2 with a bigger one, the Oldsmobile 455.

Another car lover named Jack "Doc" Watson took this idea even further. He added special paint and a Hurst gear shifter, made some changes to the engine, and put in an upscale walnut dashboard. This transformation gave birth to the Hurst/Olds.

QUICK STATS

- **Years Built**: 1968 to 1975; 1979 to 1980; 1983 to 1984
- **Maximum Hp**: 390 hp (1968)
- **0 to 60 mph (97 kmh)**: 6.2 seconds

1968 Hurst/Olds

1969 Oldsmobile Cutlass Hurst

In 1969, the Hurst/Olds got a new look. It was painted Cameo white with gold stripes and panels. It also had a big hood scoop and a rear wing.

The 1970s were a time of change. The Hurst/Olds became fancier and less powerful.

During the Hurst/Olds' production run, only about 16,000 were built. Compared to the 4-4-2, which saw 30,000 cars built in a single year, the Hurst Oldsmobile is rare.

FLEX YOUR KNOWLEDGE

The Hurst/Olds was named for George Hurst who developed automotive products. Hurst created a new kind of gear shifter that allowed drivers to move through gears faster. It was also floor-mounted. Most gear shifters were mounted on the steering column. The Hurst Shifter is still being placed in cars today. But Hurst may be best known as the inventor of a tool that helps rescue people from wrecked cars. This tool is now called the Jaws of Life.

OLDSMOBILE

1966 Toronado

TORONADO

The Oldsmobile Toronado had an interesting beginning. It all started when a designer named David North came up with an idea for a car in 1962. He called it the "Flame Red Car," but it was not something Oldsmobile planned to make.

Then, a few years later, Oldsmobile decided they wanted to create a fancy car for the 1966 model year, and they liked David North's design. To save money, they decided to use the same base, or platform, as the 1966 Buick Riviera. They decided to call the car the Toronado, which doesn't have a meaning. It was a made-up name.

QUICK STATS

- **Years Built**: 1966 to 1992
- **Maximum Hp**: 385 hp (1966)
- **0 to 60 mph (97 kmh)**: 7.5 seconds

FUN FACT

The 1966 Toronado was the first modern American car with front-wheel drive.

The 1966 Toronado was a popular model, with 40,963 cars made. The car's two doors were longer than most. This made it easier for passengers to get into the backseat. Oldsmobile also added an extra handle for the rear passenger, making it easier to open the door from inside. This feature was popular and was used in Oldsmobiles for many years.

In 1966, the Toronado won the Car of the Year from *Motor Trend* and the Award for Engineering Excellence from *Car Life*. It was even recognized in Europe, winning third place in the European Car of the Year competition that year.

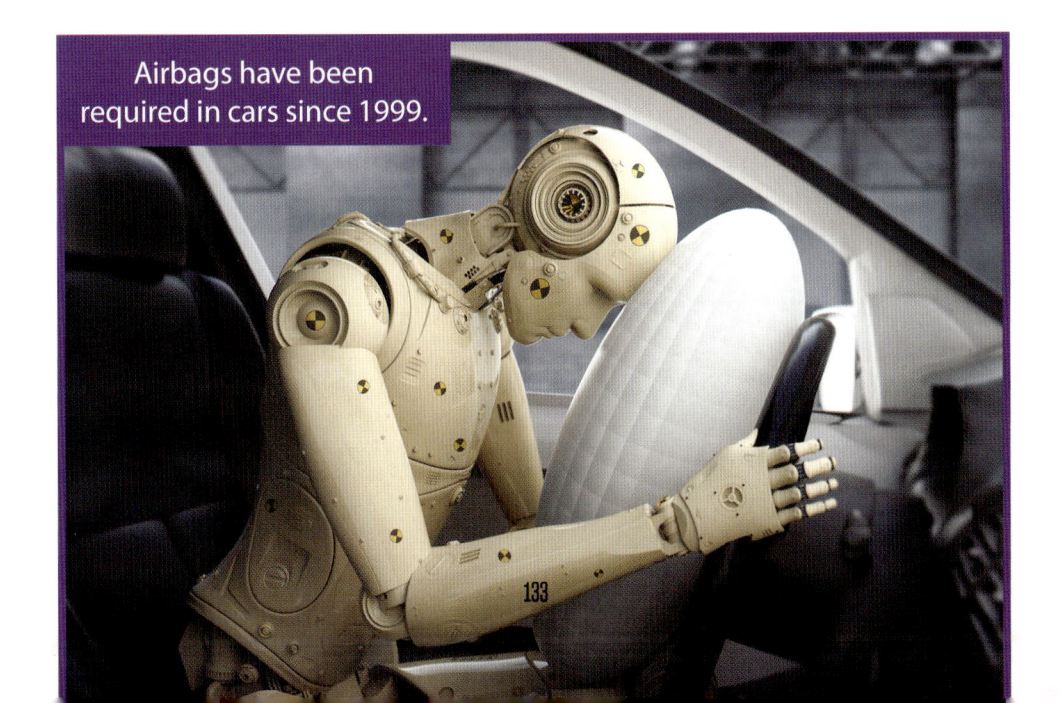

FLEX YOUR KNOWLEDGE

The airbag was invented in 1952. But the technology to sense a crash and to deploy an airbag took longer to invent. So, many carmakers did not put airbags into their cars. That is, until 1974. The Toronado was the first car to offer this feature to the public.

Airbags have been required in cars since 1999.

PLYMOUTH

In 1928, the Chrysler Corporation created a new division called Plymouth. They did this to compete with Ford and Chevrolet in the entry-level car market. An entry-level buyer is someone who is looking to purchase their first car. Most of these buyers look for lower-priced, affordable cars.

At the start, Plymouth made three low-cost cars. These were the Plymouth Four, Six, and DeLuxe Six. Even during the Great Depression, when money was tight for many people, Plymouth was able to sell these cars. The company found success.

During World War II, Plymouth made trucks and equipment for soldiers in the military. After the war, Plymouth made powerful cars like the Plymouth Belvedere and Plymouth Fury.

QUICK STATS

- **Company Headquarters**: Auburn Hills, Michigan
- **Years of Operation**: 1928 to 2001
- **Best-Selling Muscle Car**: Superbird

1960 Fury

A 1976 Road Runner burns out at the start of a drag race.

    During the 1960s and 1970s, Plymouth continued to come out with powerful cars such as the Barracuda, the Duster, and the Road Runner.

    As time went on, other car companies offered quality cars too. Plymouth had a hard time competing. People weren't buying as many Plymouth cars. In 2001, Plymouth stopped making cars.

PLYMOUTH

BARRACUDA

The Plymouth Barracuda was launched in 1964, making it one of the first muscle cars to hit the road. The Barracuda began as a version of the Plymouth Valiant, the Valiant Barracuda, but it dropped the Valiant name in 1967.

The Barracuda had a fastback design and was available with a range of V-8 engines. Models used for drag racing had extra high-performance versions of the V-8 engine.

1964 Barracuda

QUICK STATS

- **Years Built**: 1964 to 1974
- **Maximum Hp**: 182 hp (1964)
- **0 to 60 mph (97 kmh)**: 12.9 seconds

1970 'Cuda

In 1969, a high-performance Barracuda came out. It was named the 'Cuda. It had 330 horsepower in 1969, and the following year, in 1970, its horsepower jumped to 425.

Experts agree that the 1970 Barracuda was the most powerful model of this muscle car. It had 425 horsepower and a top speed of 117 miles per hour (188 kmh). It also came in some bright colors with unique names: Moulin Rouge, Sassy Grass, Vitamin C, Lemon Twist, Lime Light, and Bahama Yellow.

FUN FACT

The Barracuda was almost named the "Panda." Carmakers decided that Barracuda was a more powerful name.

PLYMOUTH

1971 Duster

DUSTER

The first-generation Duster in 1970 was made with parts from the Valiant, which was another compact Plymouth car. The Duster's body was lightweight and had a smooth sloping roof.

The fastest first-generation Dusters had a 340-cubic-inch (5.6 l) V-8 engine. In 1974 and 1975, the Duster upgraded to a 360-cubic-inch (5.9 l) V-8.

Plymouth made several unique versions of the Duster. In 1970, the Gold Duster was a special model painted gold. In 1972, buyers could get it with a reptile-patterned vinyl top. Another version, the 1972 Plymouth Duster Twister, had additional trim details and a more powerful engine. In

QUICK STATS

- **Years Built**: 1970 to 1976
- **Maximum Hp**: 275 hp (1970)
- **0 to 60 mph (97 kmh)**: 5.7 seconds

the late 1970s, Plymouth changed to meet buyers' demands for more fuel-efficient cars. They came out with the Feather Duster, which was lighter weight and had better gas mileage.

FLEX YOUR KNOWLEDGE

The Duster was a Mopar car. Mopar is a brand name that was started by the Chrysler Corporation. The name Mopar is the combination of the words "MOtor" and "PARts." The term was coined in 1937 when Chrysler introduced their own antifreeze product, which they called "MoPar Antifreeze." Later, the Mopar line included car parts and accessories. Mopar is the source for parts that go into Chrysler-owned cars.

1973 Gold Duster

PLYMOUTH

FURY

In its debut year of 1956, the Fury was a sporty and speedy mid-size sedan. It took about 16.9 seconds to cover a quarter-mile (0.4 km). It quickly became a successful NASCAR race car.

Starting in 1962, the Fury became a smaller car. It had a new grille and a slanted roofline. The Sport Fury had more upscale features like bucket seats, a padded dashboard, and a nicer steering wheel. It also had a larger, more powerful engine. The 1964 Sport Fury was one of the fastest cars Plymouth made.

QUICK STATS

- **Years Built**: 1956 to 1978
- **Maximum Hp**: 425 hp (1964)
- **0 to 60 mph (97 kmh)**: 4.9 seconds

1964 Sport Fury

1958 Fury

By 1969, when the muscle car craze was at its peak, the fifth-generation Plymouth Fury had a 440-cubic-inch (7.2 l) V-8, often called the "440 Magnum." The look of the Plymouth Fury changed in the late 1960s. It became bold and aggressive with unique grilles, hood scoops, and bold paint jobs.

Plymouth made different types of Furies. Buyers could opt for a two-door or four-door style, a hardtop, convertible, or even a station wagon.

Plymouth Fury got into racing too. Plymouth sponsored NASCAR teams, and the Fury, especially the ones with the Hemi engines, did well on the racetrack. This made the car famous as both a street and racing performer.

FLEX YOUR KNOWLEDGE

Tail fins on cars first appeared on American cars in the 1940s, but they became popular in the 1950s. Tail fins were just for looks. They did not have a purpose. Carmakers thought they would remind buyers of rockets and jets.

PLYMOUTH

GTX

Based on the Plymouth Belvedere, the GTX was one of the first Plymouth cars made just for looking sporty and going fast. When it first came out in 1967, Plymouth advertised it as the "gentleman's sports car," combining luxury with performance.

The GTX came with special black details and scoops on the hood. The hood scoops on the first year's model were faux, however. They were meant only as a stylistic feature.

The car also came with a powerful Super Commando 440 engine with 375 horsepower. The 1967 GTX could finish a quarter-mile (0.4 km) race in 14.4 seconds at 98 miles per hour (158 kmh).

FLEX YOUR KNOWLEDGE

Plymouth chose the name "GTX" as a way to compete with the Pontiac GTO. By having a similar name, Plymouth hoped to appeal to the same buyer.

1969 GTX

1970 GTX

In 1970, the Plymouth GTX got a big makeover. It looked sleeker with a new front and had an optional, and functional, extra hood scoop called "Air Grabber." New wheels and added reflective stripes along its sides helped to give the car an aggressive look. A strong engine called the "440 Six Pack" with 390 horsepower was added. Many car fans say 1970 was the best year for the GTX.

FUN FACT

The GTX came with optional racing stripes for drivers who wanted a sporty look.

QUICK STATS

- **Years Built**: 1967 to 1971
- **Maximum Hp**: 370 hp (1970)
- **0 to 60 mph (97 kmh)**: 6.5 seconds

PLYMOUTH

ROAD RUNNER

The Plymouth Road Runner is one of the most well-known muscle cars. Introduced in 1968, the Road Runner was fast and more affordable than other muscle cars at the time. It was an instant success.

From 1968 to 1970, the Road Runner had a powerful V-8 engine. In 1969, more than 84,000 cars were made due to its high demand, making 1969 the Road Runner's best year.

QUICK STATS
- **Years Built**: 1968 to 1975
- **Maximum Hp**: 425 hp (1969)
- **0 to 60 mph (97 kmh)**: 5.1 seconds

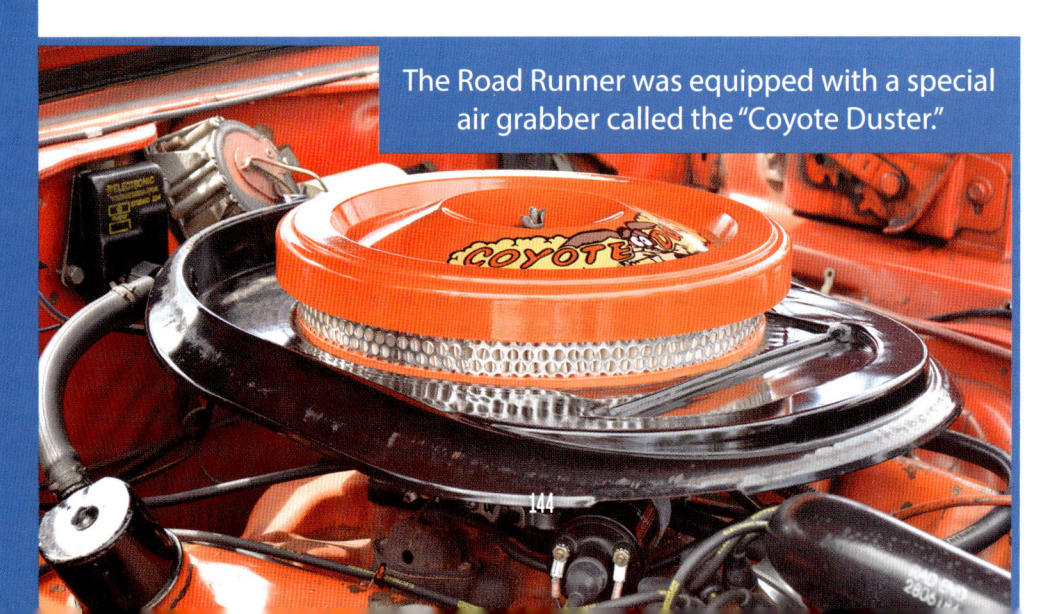

The Road Runner was equipped with a special air grabber called the "Coyote Duster."

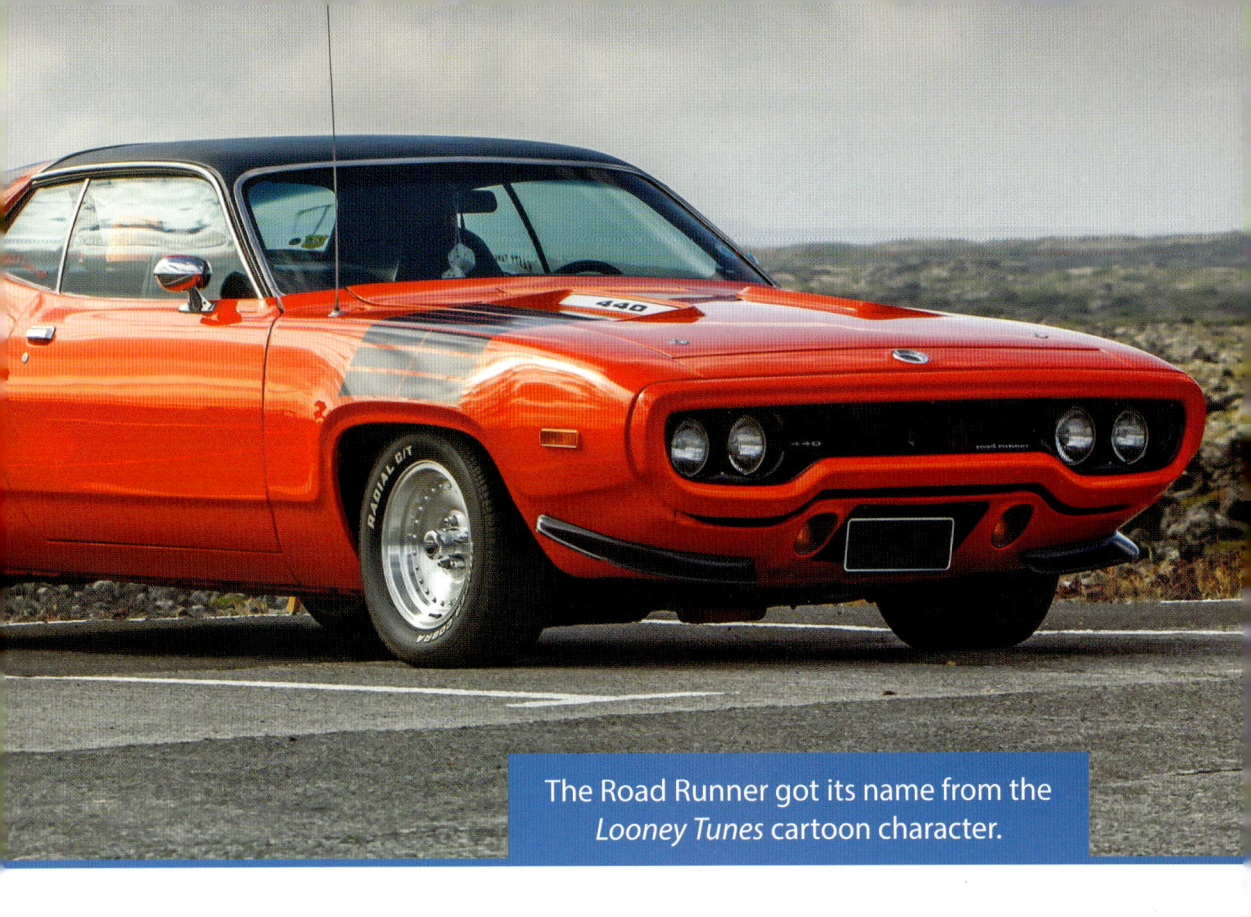

The Road Runner got its name from the *Looney Tunes* cartoon character.

From 1971 to 1974, the Road Runner went through some changes. It got bigger and heavier because of new safety and emissions laws. These changes made it a bit slower, but it still looked like its earlier models.

But then, things got tough for the Road Runner. People started liking smaller, more fuel-efficient cars because gas prices were going up. In 1975, Plymouth stopped making the Road Runner as a standalone car, but it continued being a trim option on the Volaré until 1980. That meant buyers could put some of the Road Runner features and graphics on their Volaré cars.

FUN FACT
The Plymouth Road Runner's horn made a "beep, beep" sound, just like the cartoon bird.

PLYMOUTH

1968 Satellite

SATELLITE

The Plymouth Satellite was introduced in 1965 as a mid-size car. It was based on the Plymouth Belvedere. It came with a V-8 engine. The first V-8s were called 426 wedge engines because of their shape.

The Satellite was built to look wide and boxy. The grille was stretched, and its headlights were pushed out to the corners of the car. Inside, the car had bucket seats and a center console with a space-age look to coordinate with the car's space-age name.

QUICK STATS

- **Years Built**: 1965 to 1974
- **Maximum Hp**: 390 hp (1969)
- **0 to 60 mph (97 kmh)**: 6.3 seconds

In 1966, the Satellite was offered with several V-8 engine options, including the 426 Hemi. This made the car fast on the drag strip as well as on regular roads. The Satellite also did well as a NASCAR race car.

In the late 1960s and early 1970s, the Satellite's styling changed. It was offered as a four- or two-door sedan or a wagon. A Sport Satellite option with greater horsepower was available.

The last year the Satellite was built was 1974. The car was no longer the muscle car it was in its early years. Plymouth began advertising the Satellite as a quiet car rather than as a car with a lot of power. Plymouth ads used the saying, "Built to be seen. Not heard."

FLEX YOUR KNOWLEDGE

Famous race car driver Richard Petty won two NASCAR Grand National races and a Winston Cup Championship driving a Satellite.

PLYMOUTH

SUPERBIRD

In the late 1960s, Plymouth's parent company, Chrysler, wanted to dominate NASCAR. But Ford had cars like the Torino Talladega and the Mercury Cyclone Spoiler II, which kept winning races. Then in 1968, Plymouth lost their star NASCAR race car driver Richard Petty to Ford because he liked their cars better. To get their star driver back and to further compete with Ford, Plymouth introduced the Superbird in 1970. The Superbird was fast. It could hit the quarter-mile (0.4 km) mark in 13.5 seconds. But what was most unusual was its shape. The Superbird had a pointy nose, a slanted rear window, and, like the Charger Daytona, a big wing on the back, which gave the car better aerodynamics and handling.

FUN FACT

The Superbird was a highly modified version of the Road Runner. Their interiors were nearly identical, and, like the Road Runner's horn, the Superbird's also went "beep, beep."

QUICK STATS

- **Year Built**: 1970
- **Maximum Hp**: 425 hp (1970)
- **0 to 60 mph (97 kmh)**: 4.8 seconds

1970 Superbird

With the legendary Richard Petty back on the Plymouth team and behind the wheel, the car won 18 NASCAR races in 1970. In most races, the car hit speeds of more than 200 miles per hour (322 kmh).

Soon, Plymouth started selling the Superbird to ordinary drivers. However, laws about racing and about engine sizes changed. As a result, the Superbird was made for just one year, and only 1,935 were made. Today, these cars are very rare.

FLEX YOUR KNOWLEDGE

Chrysler's two winged cars, the Superbird and the Charger Daytona, dominated NASCAR in 1969 and 1970. But in 1970, NASCAR created new rules that limited engine size. The aerodynamics that come with a rear wing work best at very fast speeds. But because cars couldn't go as fast with smaller engines, the wing became ineffective. It was no longer used.

PLYMOUTH

VALIANT

The Valiant debuted in 1959 as a small, reliable, and affordable car. In 1963, the Signet was introduced as Valiant's high-end version with features such as bucket seats and interior carpeting.

Following the muscle-car trend, Plymouth increased the Valiant's power and performance in the mid-1960s. It was no longer just small and inexpensive; it also had powerful engines for people who wanted speed. The Valiant Barracuda was a fast version created in 1964. In 1967, the Barracuda spun off to create its own line of cars. But the Valiant continued on as its own car model.

1968 Valiant Signet

QUICK STATS

- **Years Built**: 1959 to 1976
- **Maximum Hp**: 230 hp (1968)
- **0 to 60 mph (97 kmh)**: 7.9 seconds

1969 Valiant

In 1970, a new version of the Valiant was created. It was the Valiant Duster. Like the Barracuda before it, the Duster spun off into its own line of vehicles the following year. To replace the Duster model, the Scamp became the Valiant's next variation.

In the early 1970s, Plymouth had to deal with new rules about safety and pollution. To follow these rules, changes were made including adding a large front bumper for better protection. In addition, smaller, more fuel-saving engines became common as the car changed with the times. Sales began to drop, however, and in 1976, Plymouth stopped making the Valiant.

FLEX YOUR KNOWLEDGE

Dodge and Plymouth were considered sister companies since they were both owned by the same parent company, Chrysler. As a result, many of their cars were alike, sharing the same chassis design, engines, and transmissions. The Dodge Dart and the Plymouth Valiant were essentially the same car but with differently designed bodies and trim details.

PONTIAC

The Pontiac company did not begin with cars. It began with buggies. In 1893, Edward Murphy created the Pontiac Buggy Company, which built horse-drawn carriages. But in 1907, Murphy switched to making cars. He changed the company's name to the Oakland Motor Car Company. Just two years later in 1909, General Motors bought the company, eventually changing the company's name back to Pontiac.

In 1926, Pontiac introduced a new kind of car called the "Chief of the Sixes." These cars were powered by six-cylinder engines. Most cars in that time only had four cylinders.

In the 1930s, Pontiac began making their cars with a style called Silver Streak. The cars had metal bands that ran down the middle of the hoods to the grilles, giving the cars a distinctive look.

1939 Silver Streak

FUN FACT
Pontiac was named after an Ottawa chief who lived in the Great Lakes area in the 1700s.

The first Pontiac logo

1964 GTO

In 1964, the Pontiac GTO was introduced. Many people consider the GTO to be the first true muscle car. It was stylish, powerful, and not too expensive. The GTO became one of the most famous muscle cars.

Because of money troubles in the car industry, General Motors decided to stop making Pontiac cars. The last Pontiac cars were built in 2010.

FLEX YOUR KNOWLEDGE

Headquartered in Detroit, Michigan, General Motors is a large automotive company that owns and builds several brands of cars including Chevrolet, Buick, and Pontiac.

QUICK STATS

- **Company Headquarters**: Detroit, Michigan
- **Years of Operation**: 1926 to 2010
- **Best-Selling Muscle Car**: GTO

BONNEVILLE

The Pontiac Bonneville was named after the Bonneville Salt Flats in Utah, a famous site for setting land speed records. The 1957 Bonneville was the first-generation Bonneville. At the time, it was the fastest Pontiac ever produced.

The 1959 Bonneville was a wide track car, which made it steadier and easier to handle than other cars. It had a powerful engine and a bold front end with a split grille. Along with the Pontiac GTO, the Bonneville was considered an early muscle car.

FLEX YOUR KNOWLEDGE

The Bonneville Salt Flats is a large, flat area filled with hard-packed salt. The salt was left behind as an ancient lake dried up. Since the early 1900s, it has become an area famous for racing cars, motorcycles, and other vehicles.

QUICK STATS

- **Years Built**: 1957 to 2005
- **Maximum Hp**: 315 hp (1957)
- **0 to 60 mph (97 kmh)**: 8.1 seconds

1960s Bonneville

In the 1960s, the Bonneville was still a large sedan, but its design became more streamlined. Larger engines produced greater horsepower and faster speeds.

The 1970 Pontiac Bonneville had a unique look that was a mix of sharp angles and a strong appearance. Even though it was big like previous models, it also had a modern look that matched the time.

The last year that the Pontiac Bonneville still had some muscle car qualities was in 1970. After that, the Bonneville evolved to be more about luxury and style.

FUN FACT

The Bonneville was one of Pontiac's largest sedans. Some people called them "land yachts," not only because of their size but also because they were good for cruising around town.

PONTIAC

1962 Catalina

CATALINA

Pontiac introduced the Catalina in 1959 as a full-size car, but it wasn't until the 1962 Catalina Super Duty that this car was considered a muscle car.

The 1962 Catalina Super Duty was built to race in NASCAR. With a powerful 421 big block V-8 engine, the car could have gained a huge following. But since it was intended for racing, it was not widely available for sale. Pontiac only made around 162 Catalinas during all of 1962.

QUICK STATS

- **Years Built**: 1959 to 1981
- **Maximum Hp**: 405 hp (1963)
- **0 to 60 mph (97 kmh)**: 5.5 seconds

When NASCAR officials learned about the Super Duty's big engine, new rules were made. Race cars had to use parts that could be placed in regular, non-racing cars.

In order to follow the rules, Pontiac put the same engine in around 180 cars. Some of these cars belong to lucky collectors today.

FLEX YOUR KNOWLEDGE

The 2+2 package was an upgrade for the Catalina car made for people who liked to drive fast but also wanted a comfortable ride. The 2+2 included a strong V-8 engine and a tough suspension. It also offered bucket seats and customized paint and striping details.

1963 Catalina

PONTIAC

FIREBIRD

In 1967, Pontiac introduced the first Firebird. It was built to compete with Pontiac's rivals, the Ford Mustang and the Chevy Camaro, on the racetrack and in the showroom. The Firebird quickly became popular.

The fastest model in its debut year was the Firebird 400. It had a ram air system with special scoops on the hood that brought in cold air for more power and faster acceleration.

QUICK STATS

- **Years Built**: 1967 to 2002
- **Maximum Hp**: 335 hp (1969)
- **0 to 60 mph (97 kmh)**: 6.2 seconds

1969 Firebird

1966 Firebird

The fastest engine available in the 1967 Pontiac Firebird was the 400-cubic-inch (6.6 l) V-8 engine. It produced around 325 horsepower and 430 lbs-ft of torque. This made it one of the most powerful models that year. But the Firebird never broke 400 horsepower, like its competitors. The 1969 Firebird had the most with 335 horsepower. Pontiac instead focused on handling and design.

In 1969, the look of the front of the Firebird changed. The headlights were separated by the grille, and a different bumper was added. The idea was to make the car not only look muscular but also to be different from the Camaro, which had a similar look.

FUN FACT

In the 1970s, a decal was added to the hood of the Firebird. It was nicknamed the Screaming Chicken. Firebirds were easily recognized by this famous and popular decal.

PONTIAC

1978 Firebird Trans Am

In 1969, Pontiac introduced a new package for the Firebird: the Trans Am. The Firebird Trans Am had the same power as the other models, but it was designed to look more aggressive and tougher than the original Firebird.

Even though laws were changing in the early 1970s, Pontiac released one of its most powerful Trans Ams, the Trans Am Super Duty, in 1973. It came with a 455-cubic-inch (7.5 l) V-8 engine known as the Super Duty 455. It was highly tuned to reach maximum horsepower of 310.

FLEX YOUR KNOWLEDGE

Tuning a car means making modifications to help improve its performance or handling. To make a car faster or more powerful, the engine can be modified with different or added parts, such as larger cylinders or turbochargers. Changing parts of a car's suspension or lowering the car's body can help it handle better on the road.

In 1977, Pontiac made a special edition Firebird to celebrate its 50th anniversary. The Firebird was painted black and gold. These cars also had T-tops with removable panels. They were the first Firebirds to have them.

The Pontiac Firebird continued to be made until 2002. But its most popular year was 1978. Pontiac sold more Firebirds that year than any other. This might be because a year earlier, in 1977, the movie *Smokey and the Bandit* came out. This popular movie starred famous actor Burt Reynolds who drove a Firebird. After the movie, demand for the car increased.

FUN FACT

The Firebird used in *Smokey and the Bandit* was actually a combination of two Firebirds: a 1976 model with a 1977 front end.

1977 Firebird

PONTIAC

GRAND AM

The Grand Am was introduced in 1973, at the tail end of the muscle car years. The car combined the luxury of the Pontiac Grand Prix with the performance of the Trans Am.

The Grand Am's grille was divided into six sections with vertical bars, which is sometimes called a "catwalk" grille. It also had a unique nose, which was called the Endura nose. Instead of a typical bumper, its nose was made of a material that could bounce back into shape after a low-speed bump.

To compete with European carmakers such as BMW, Pontiac gave the Grand Am an upscale interior. The car was outfitted with bucket seats, a nice-looking dashboard, and a wood-trimmed console. Pontiac even copied the note of the European car horn, which was a higher note than other Pontiacs.

1973 Grand Am

FLEX YOUR KNOWLEDGE

Disc brakes use friction to slow and stop cars. They have three main parts: a metal plate, called a brake disc or rotor, which is attached to the wheel; a clamp, called the brake caliper, which holds the brake pads; and the pads themselves.

The 1973 Grand Am had front disc brakes. Disc brakes were invented in the early 1900s, but they were not standard in GM cars until 1973. Disc brakes were safer and more effective than drum or hydraulic brakes.

Sales of the first generation of the Grand Am slipped in 1974, most likely due to emissions standards. Pontiac stopped making it in 1975. A second generation was built in 1978, but it did not do well. The Grand Am was reintroduced in 1985 as a more family-friendly sedan. It was built until 2005.

QUICK STATS

- **Years Built**: 1973 to 1975; 1978 to 1980; 1985 to 2005
- **Maximum Hp**: 310 hp (1973)
- **0 to 60 mph (97 kmh)**: 6.4 seconds

PONTIAC

GRAND PRIX

Debuting in 1962, the Grand Prix was a speedy luxury car that was built to compete with the Ford Thunderbird. It originally came out as a coupe with a long body and a big hood. But its style changed over the years.

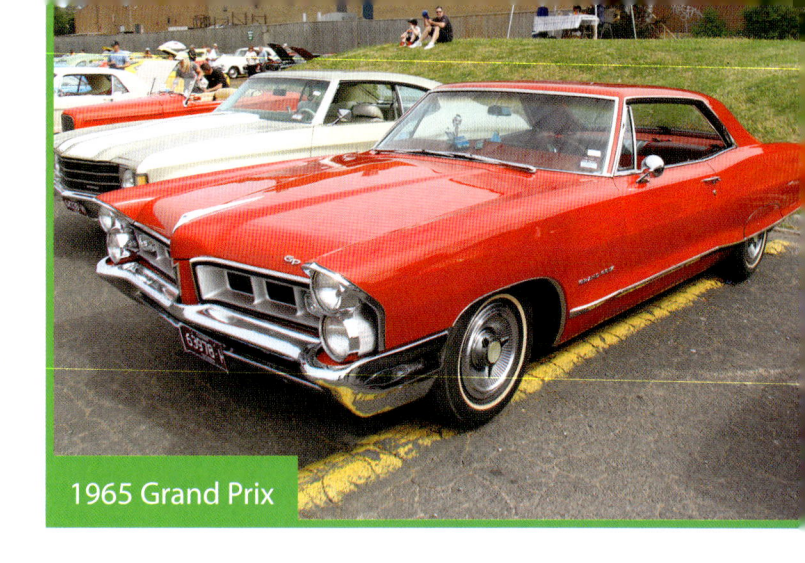

1965 Grand Prix

The 1965 Grand Prix had a squared-off roofline and a divided grille. Two headlights were on either side of the grille, and they were stacked rather than side by side. Its windshield was larger than most, making for better visibility on the road. It had an automatic transmission with three speeds, making it easy to drive. Some also had a manual transmission for better control when shifting gears.

Like most muscle cars, the Grand Prix used power from the back wheels, making it handle well and feel sporty. The car was not fuel efficient, however. The car only got 11 miles per gallon (18 km per 4 l). Even so, 1965 was a very good year for Pontiac. The Grand Prix was one of its best-selling cars.

QUICK STATS

- **Years Built**: 1962 to 2002 (coupes); 1989 to 2008 (sedans)
- **Maximum Hp**: 390 hp (1969)
- **0 to 60 mph (97 kmh)**: 6.8 seconds

By 1969, the coke-bottle design of the Grand Prix became more prominent. It kept its long hood, but it now had a V-shaped grille, square headlights, and a more rounded back end. Like other Pontiacs, it was considered a luxurious and comfortable muscle car on the inside. It had bucket seats and an interior panel that was angled toward the driver. This made it easier to reach knobs and buttons.

But like other Grand Prix models before it, what made this 1969 model special was its powerful engine. It was a heavy car, but it could accelerate quickly. Many consider the Grand Prix one of the best sleeper cars of the 1960s.

FUN FACT
A "sleeper" is a nickname for a car that has an exterior that isn't flashy but is fast and powerful. Other drivers might not expect a sleeper car to perform as well as it does.

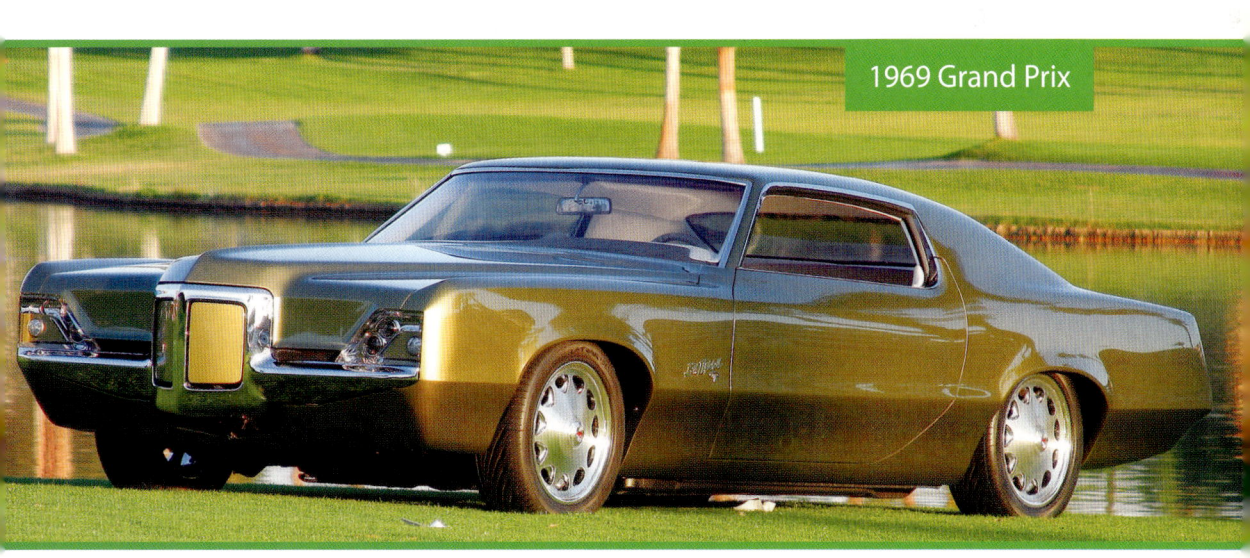

1969 Grand Prix

PONTIAC

GTO

In 1963, a group of Pontiac engineers led by John Z. DeLorean realized they could fit the bigger and more powerful 389-cubic-inch (6.4 l) V-8 engine from the Bonneville into the new midsize Tempest. A week later, they had a prototype for one of the most famous muscle cars, the 1964 Pontiac GTO.

DeLorean named his creation the GTO. The name was borrowed from the famous Italian carmaker Ferrari. While some people on the street believed GTO meant "Gas, Tires, and Oil," it actually stood for *Gran Turismo Omologato*, which means "Grand Touring Homologated."

FLEX YOUR KNOWLEDGE

Many races, like NASCAR, had a rule that in order for a car to race, the model had to be homologated. That means there needed to be enough cars made that it could be sold to the public. For most races during the classic muscle car era, at least 500 cars had to be made to be considered homologated.

QUICK STATS

- **Years Built**: 1963 to 1974; 2004 to 2006
- **Maximum Hp**: 360 hp (1968)
- **0 to 60 mph (97 kmh)**: 6.6 seconds

1968 GTO

The 1964 GTO was an instant hit. Pontiac sold more than 30,000 in the car's first year. Only 5,000 were expected to sell. For the 1965 and 1966 GTOs, a Ram Air kit was added. In addition, Pontiac replaced the faux hood scoop with one that was functional. Starting in 1967, GTO models came with open scoops on the hood. These scoops cost extra. Only 751 of these models were made.

Nearly 100,000 GTOs were sold in 1966, making it one of the most popular muscle cars in history. From 1964 to 1966, the GTO dominated the muscle car market while others played catch-up. However, competition heated up in 1967 when the Chevy Camaro, Oldsmobile 4-4-2, and Dodge Coronet R/T were introduced.

PONTIAC

In 1968, the GTO received a makeover that included hidden headlights, which were an option for only two years. The GTO also had a bumper made of sturdy Endura rubber that matched its color. The Endura bumper was used on future Pontiacs, including the Grand Am and the Firebird.

Pontiac never built a GTO with more than 400 horsepower. The most powerful GTOs of the classic muscle car era were the 1969 and 1970 models that had 370 horsepower.

FLEX YOUR KNOWLEDGE

The GTO had several nicknames. Many people called it the "GOAT." Goats are known to eat anything, and the nickname referred to its ability to "eat" other cars and beat them in a race. Others say that GOAT stands for "greatest of all time." Besides the GOAT, the GTO had other nicknames as well. They included "The Tiger," "The Great One," and "The Humbler."

1969 GTO, "The Judge"

The Judge was created in 1969 as a budget GTO, designed for street racing. This model lasted for three years.

By 1974, the GTO was no longer considered a muscle car. It didn't have the horsepower or acceleration of its previous models. Pontiac revived the GTO in 2004. While some of the GTOs in 2005 and 2006 were fast with 400 horsepower, the GTO looked nothing like the car of the 1960s and early 1970s. It did not sell well. The last year Pontiac made the GTO was 2006.

PONTIAC

VENTURA

The Pontiac Ventura was a name given to different types of cars that Pontiac made from 1960 to 1979. It first began as a special trim option for the Pontiac Catalina. It was meant to be a fancier version of the car.

In 1967, Pontiac introduced a new version of the Ventura. It was no longer a type of Catalina. Instead, it became its own type of car in the Pontiac family. The newer Ventura had a sporty look, with sleek lines and chrome accents.

1960 Ventura

1972 Ventura

From 1971 to 1979, Pontiac made the next generations of the Ventura. The 1974 Pontiac added GTO to the Ventura's name to give it a muscle-car feel. The Ventura GTO was a small-sized car. It didn't have as much power as muscle cars built in the 1960s, but because it was lighter than other muscle cars, it still was fast.

By then, buyers wanted to save money on gas. The Ventura Pontiac could drive 20 miles for every gallon (32 km per 4 l). That was considered good fuel economy for the time, making the car attractive to buyers.

QUICK STATS

- **Years Built:** 1960 to 1979
- **Maximum Hp:** 200 hp (1974)
- **0 to 60 mph (97 kmh):** 7.9 seconds

FUN FACT

The Ventura car was named after the city Ventura, located in Southern California. The word *ventura* comes from the Italian term "bona-venture," which means "good fortune."

CULTURE

Muscle cars are much more than just loud and powerful cars. They have become part of American culture. During the height of the muscle car era, they became symbols of freedom. With powerful engines and speed, muscle cars gave people a sense that the world is one big open road full of possibilities.

Speed and power weren't the only appealing features of muscle cars. The design, colors, and price were all geared for young buyers too.

Pony cars, such as the Ford Mustang, were a smaller and more affordable type of muscle car. These cars were designed to be fast and fun, attracting a whole new generation of drivers. Pony cars had their own enthusiasts and followers.

1969 Chevrolet Camaro SS

1960s Ford Mustang

As muscle cars became more popular, they began playing a larger role in American culture, especially in movies and in television shows. Fast, loud, stylish cars made for exciting car chases and car races. In turn, popular movies and television shows made owning a muscle car even more desirable.

Since the end of the classic muscle car era, the muscle car culture has continued to grow. Muscle cars bring a sense of nostalgia for those who owned one when they were younger. In addition, muscle cars have a strong following among car collectors. Car shows provide the opportunity to gather, to share tips and ideas, and to show off cars and collections. Many car owners enjoy restoring their old cars. Some restored muscle cars from the 1960s and 1970s are still raced in vintage car races.

RACING

Muscle cars have played an important role in the culture of auto racing. They are known for their power and fast acceleration, but many, especially early models, did not have great handling. They didn't move smoothly around turns and corners, but they could move well in a straight line.

Muscle cars were popular in illegal street racing, which began to grow in the 1960s. Drivers pitted their cars against one another to prove their car's power. Rivalries often developed between drivers, car clubs, or different car models.

Sadly, there were many crashes, injuries, and fatalities. Street racing's dangers, however, led to the established, legal sport of drag racing. Drag strips and racetracks provide drivers with a safer, controlled environment for their passion.

Muscle cars compete in a drag race.

Muscle cars have also played an important role in NASCAR. Many street-legal muscle cars were born from NASCAR-designed cars, such as the Dodge Daytona. With homologation rules in place, carmakers were required to make their NASCAR cars available to the public to purchase. This not only made those cars more popular, but it also helped make all muscle cars popular. A buyer might not have had the means to purchase a street-legal Dodge Daytona, but a Dodge Charger might have been within the budget.

Wins from famous race car drivers such as Richard Petty helped spur the popularity of muscle cars.

CUSTOMIZATION

In the 1960s and 1970s, many people customized their muscle cars. They added special features to make their cars stand out and perform even better.

One way to customize their muscle cars was by giving them a fresh coat of paint. Bright colors such as neon green, fiery red, or electric blue were popular. To make the cars even more exciting, racing stripes were sometimes added.

The addition of graphics and decals helped make a muscle car look even more unique. Tinted windows added a feeling of mystery and could make a car look tough.

People customized their engines by adding things like bigger carburetors and high-performance exhaust systems. Superchargers forced more air into the engine to make it go faster.

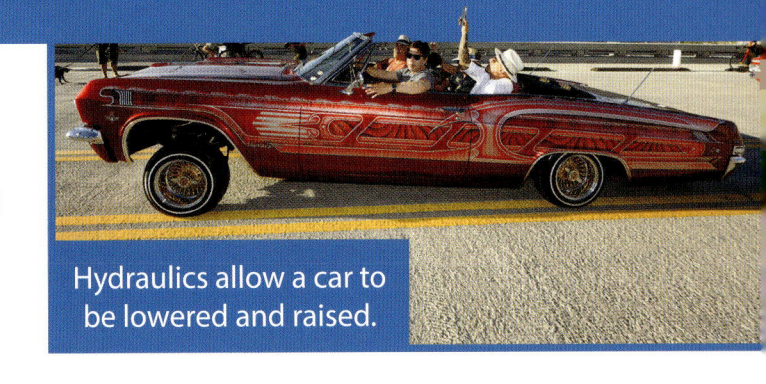

Hydraulics allow a car to be lowered and raised.

Drivers sometimes customized their tires too. Bigger tires not only looked tough, but they also gave the car more grip on the road. Some people replaced their regular-sized tires with smaller ones. This lowered the car, giving it better handling and a different look.

Today, car enthusiasts and collectors continue to customize and restore their muscle cars. Over the years, this has resulted in a booming after-market industry.

1971 Chevrolet Chevelle

FLEX YOUR KNOWLEDGE

Racing stripes began as a way for fans to tell cars apart on the racetracks. In the 1950s, race teams used colors that represented their countries. Now, stripes are added to cars to make them look cool and fast.

CAR SHOWS

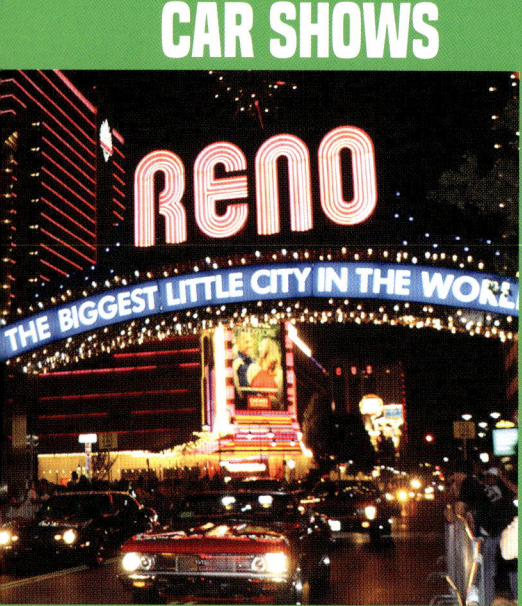

Hot August Nights is a car show in Reno, Nevada.

Muscle car shows are events where people get together to enjoy and show off muscle cars. The Woodward Dream Cruise is one of the most iconic automotive events in the world. It takes place every summer in Detroit, Michigan. Located on a 16-mile (26 km) stretch of Woodward Avenue, the event attracts thousands of classic cars, muscle cars, hot rods, and other unique vehicles.

For this rolling car show, participants and spectators line the streets to watch and interact with the vehicles as they cruise up and down the street. There are also various car clubs, vendors, live music performances, and entertainment.

FUN FACT
The Woodward Dream Cruise is the world's largest one-day automotive event.

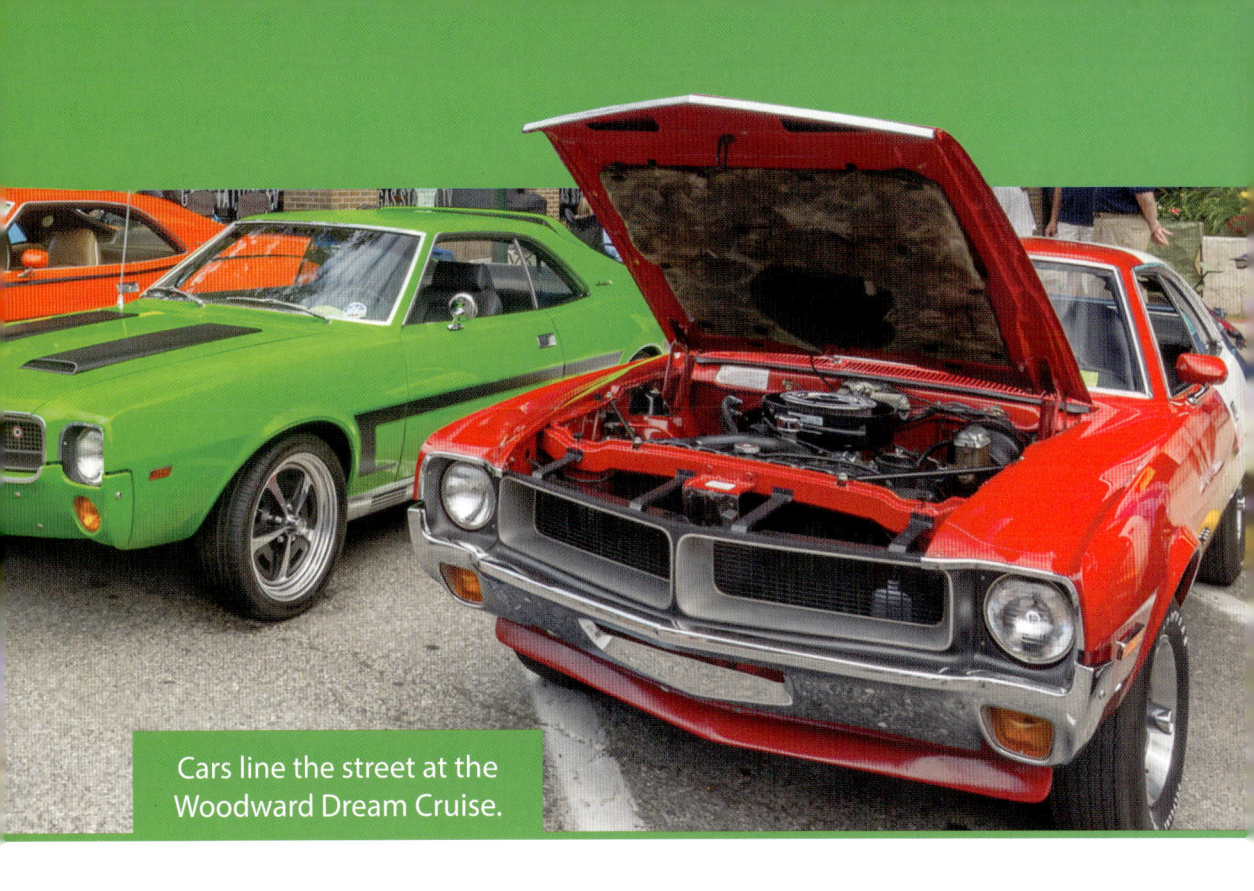

Cars line the street at the Woodward Dream Cruise.

The Iola Old Car Show is an annual event held in Iola, Wisconsin, that celebrates classic and vintage automobiles. It started in 1972 as a small gathering of antique car enthusiasts and has grown into one of the largest car shows of its kind in the United States. It features not only vehicle displays but also swap meets, car auctions, a large car parts marketplace, and various entertainment options, including live music and food vendors.

Hot August Nights features cars from the 1950s and 1960s. Millions of people come to see the cars on display and as they cruise by. There are also car auctions, live music shows, and drag races.

MODERN MUSCLE CARS

2005 Mustang GT

QUICK STATS: FORD MUSTANG GT
- **Years Built**: 2005 to 2009
- **Maximum Hp**: 300 hp (2005)
- **0 to 60 mph (97 kmh)**: 4.9 seconds

The classic muscle car era of the 1960s and early 1970s was cut short, mostly due to an oil shortage and rising gas prices combined with new rules about emissions. Carmakers had to quickly redesign their vehicles to meet new demands.

But in the 2000s, the muscle car made a comeback. Demand for high-performance, powerful vehicles was on the rise. People also began looking for cars that reminded them of muscle cars of the past. As technology improved, carmakers were able to build cars that could give buyers the style and performance they were looking for while also meeting modern emissions standards.

In 2005, Ford introduced the fifth generation of the Mustang. It had a retro design and a powerful engine with modern technology. The car renewed buyers' passion for muscle cars. With the Mustang's success, other carmakers followed Ford's lead and began building modern muscle cars.

In 2006, Dodge introduced a new Charger and, in 2008, the next generation of the Challenger came out. Like the 2005 Mustang, the Challenger had a retro design, along with a Hemi V-8 engine. In 2010, Chevrolet brought out its new Camaro. The revival of the muscle car had begun. And so had the competition for building the best one.

2010 Chevrolet Camaro

MUSCLE CARS OF THE 2000S

2007 FORD SHELBY MUSTANG GT500

In 2007, Ford and Shelby teamed up once again to build a car together. The Shelby Mustang GT500 was based on the 2005 Mustang GT. But this version took the car to a new level in style and performance. The original Shelby GT500, introduced in 1967, did the same thing for the non-Shelby Mustang.

QUICK STATS
- **Years Built**: 2007 to 2009
- **Maximum Hp**: 500 hp (2007)
- **0 to 60 mph (97 kmh)**: 4.5 seconds

FUN FACT
In 2007, the Shelby GT500 was the most powerful Mustang ever built by Ford.

2007 Shelby GT500

2005 PONTIAC GTO

In the 2000s, Pontiac brought back the GTO. But the newer version did not have the same look as its famous version from the 1960s. Many people thought its design was too ordinary, but it had the power of a muscle car. It was one of the fastest cars of the 2000s.

QUICK STATS

- **Years Built:** 2004 to 2006
- **Maximum Hp:** 400 hp (2005)
- **0 to 60 mph (97 kmh):** 4.7 seconds

2005 GTO

2006 DODGE CHARGER SRT8

In the 2000s, Dodge introduced the sixth generation of the Charger. The 2006 Charger was a four-door muscle car. It could move fast, especially for a big car. In fact, it was the quickest highway-legal car Dodge had ever made up to that time.

QUICK STATS

- **Years Built:** 2006 to 2010
- **Maximum Hp:** 425 hp (2006)
- **0 to 60 mph (97 kmh):** 5 seconds

2006 Charger SRT8

MUSCLE CARS OF THE 2010S

2012 FORD MUSTANG BOSS 302

Ford built the first Mustang Boss 302 in 1969. In 2012, Ford redesigned it and brought it back. The 2012 version was built with more advanced technology and a more comfortable interior than the original. But it kept the same color options: orange, white, blue, yellow, or red. The car also kept the same stripes that run along the sides and roof.

QUICK STATS

- **Years Built**: 2012 to 2014
- **Maximum Hp**: 440 hp (2012)
- **0 to 60 mph (97 kmh)**: 4 seconds

2012 Mustang Boss 302

2016 CHEVROLET CAMARO SS

In 2016, the sixth generation of the Camaro was introduced. Aluminum was used to make some of its parts. That made it 200 pounds (91 kg) lighter than the fifth-generation models, making it quicker and more fuel efficient.

QUICK STATS

- **Years Built**: 2016 to present
- **Maximum Hp**: 455 hp (2017)
- **0 to 60 mph (97 kmh)**: 4 seconds

2016 Camaro SS

DODGE CHALLENGER AND CHARGER HELLCATS

Dodge debuted its Challenger and Charger Hellcats in 2015. The cars were named after the Grumman F6F Hellcat, a World War II plane known for its power. When the Challenger Hellcat was released, it was the most powerful muscle car ever made. During its first year of production, Dodge sold out of Challenger Hellcats within just five days.

QUICK STATS

- **Years Built:** 2015 to 2023
- **Maximum Hp:** 707 hp (2017)
- **0 to 60 mph (97 kmh):** 3.5 seconds (Challenger); 3.4 seconds (Charger)

2017 Charger Hellcat

DODGE CHALLENGER SRT DEMON

The Dodge Challenger SRT Demon was one of the fastest and most powerful cars of the 2010s. When it came out in 2018, it was more powerful than the Hellcat, becoming the new most powerful muscle car ever. The Demon could go a quarter-mile (0.4 km) in fewer than 10 seconds.

QUICK STATS

- **Years Built:** 2018
- **Maximum Hp:** 840 hp (2018)
- **0 to 60 mph (97 kmh):** 2.4 seconds

2018 Challenger SRT Demon

MUSCLE CARS OF THE 2020S AND BEYOND

In the 2020s, more cars began using alternative fuels, such as electricity, to be more earth-friendly. But buyers continue to want power and speed. Carmakers are using new approaches in design to meet these demands. Advances in technology allow cars to be more fuel efficient. Newer cars are also being made with special materials that are strong but also very light. This makes the cars go fast and use less fuel.

Advanced technology continues to make drivers safer and more comfortable. Infotainment systems, touchscreens, and high-end audio systems are common. Safety features such as external cameras, auto parking, and emergency braking assistance are becoming standard. These advances will continue to improve.

One such improvement may be in autonomous driving. But feeling the power and speed behind the wheel is one of a muscle car's most appealing features. Many muscle car drivers may not want to let the car drive itself.

2024 Corvette E-Ray

Muscle cars have gained fans over many decades and across many generations. Regardless of how muscle cars evolve in the future, they will still be all about power, speed, style, and a sense of freedom.

2024 CORVETTE E-RAY

The E-Ray is the first all-wheel drive Corvette. It's also the first hybrid Corvette. This car is more environmentally friendly than gas-only vehicles. When in stealth mode, the E-Ray runs on the electric motor only, which enables it to drive nearly silently.

QUICK STATS

- **Years Built:** 2024 to present
- **Maximum Hp:** 655 hp (2024)
- **0 to 60 mph (97 kmh):** 2.5 seconds

2024 CAMARO ZL1

The Camaro ZL1 was built for performance and style, not for practicality. There are no back seats, and its trunk space is small. It does have a lot of modern technology, though, including wireless connectivity, infotainment and upscale audio systems, and safety and driver-assistance features.

QUICK STATS

- **Years Built:** 2019 to present
- **Maximum Hp:** 650 hp (2024)
- **0 to 60 mph (97 kmh):** 3.4 seconds

Camaro ZL1

GLOSSARY

accelerate
To go faster or increase speed.

aerodynamic
Able to move through air easily.

chassis
The supporting frame or structure of a car.

Cold War
A period of tension between the Soviet Union and the United States that started after World War II and lasted until the early 1990s; called the Cold War because the two countries never actually fought each other directly.

combustion
Describes an engine that gets its energy from the burning of fuel.

compress
To press or squeeze together.

coupe
A type of car that is usually smaller than regular cars and has two doors instead of four.

debuted
When something is shown to the public for the first time.

embargo
An order by a government that prevents trade or business with another country.

exhaust
The escape system for gases leaving a vehicle.

fastback
A style of making cars where the back part of the car slopes down smoothly and quickly.

faux
Not real, fake.

horsepower
A way to measure the power of an engine or a machine.

iconic
Something that is famous and well-known and is easily recognized by many people.

infotainment
Programming or technology that provides information as well as entertainment.

nostalgia
A longing for the past or something in the past.

prototype
The first model of a new design on which others are patterned.

spoiler
A device that interrupts airflow over the body of a car as it moves, giving it better aerodynamics.

suspension
A system of springs and shock absorbers that helps the car ride smoothly, even on bumpy roads.

transmission
The parts of the car that reduce or increase the speed and power of the engine.

vintage
Something that is old in a special and valuable way.

TO LEARN MORE

FURTHER READINGS

Farr, Donald. *The Complete Book of Classic Ford and Mercury Muscle Cars: 1961–1973*. Chartwell, 2023.

Mighty Muscle Cars Series. Abdo, 2021.

Muscle Cars: Marvels of Power and Performance. Publications International, Ltd., 2023.

ONLINE RESOURCES

Booklinks NONFICTION NETWORK
FREE! ONLINE NONFICTION RESOURCES

To learn more about muscle cars, please visit **abdobooklinks.com** or scan this QR code. These links are routinely monitored and updated to provide the most current information available.

INDEX

4-4-2 12, 22, 126, 127, 128, 129, 130, 131, 167
24 Hours of Le Mans 98, 99

aerodynamics 15, 80, 81, 112, 125, 148, 149, 188
AMX 20, 24, 25, 26, 27, 28

Barracuda 6, 23, 74, 101, 135, 136, 137, 150, 151
Bel Air 42, 44, 45, 46, 47, 62
Biscayne 48, 49
Bonneville 154, 155, 166

Camaro 8, 12, 13, 19, 20, 42, 43, 50, 51, 52, 53, 76, 158, 159, 167, 172, 181, 184, 187
Capri 92, 93
Carroll Shelby 6, 23, 98, 104, 106
Catalina 156, 157, 170
Challenger 6, 15, 19, 21, 72, 73, 74, 75, 181, 185
Charger 12, 72, 73, 76, 77, 78, 79, 80, 81, 89, 112, 148, 149, 175, 181, 183, 185
Charger Daytona 78, 80, 81, 148, 149
Chevelle 6, 7, 8, 12, 21, 43, 54, 55, 66, 112, 177
Chrysler 25, 72, 80, 134, 139, 148, 149, 151
coke-bottle design 165
Comet 116, 118, 119, 122
Coronet 82, 83, 86, 167
Corvette 39, 43, 56, 57, 58, 59, 108, 186, 187
Cougar 8, 116, 117, 120, 121
Cyclone 118, 122, 123, 148

Dart 84, 85, 151
drag racing 8, 37, 48, 52, 77, 82, 96, 121, 136, 174
Duster 135, 138, 139, 144, 151

El Camino 43, 60, 61
emissions 53, 145, 163, 180

Fairlane 54, 94, 95, 112
fastback 23, 26, 59, 66, 97, 102, 123, 136, 188
Firebird 19, 158, 159, 160, 161, 168
Fury 134, 140, 141

Galaxie 91, 96, 97
Grand Am 162, 163, 168
Grand National 38, 39, 46, 47, 123, 147
Grand Prix 162, 164, 165
Gran Sport 34, 36, 37
GT40 98, 99
GTO 5, 12, 13, 22, 23, 128, 142, 153, 154, 166, 167, 168, 169, 171, 183
GTX 142, 143

Hemi engines 78, 141
hood scoop 17, 29, 68, 87, 131, 143, 167
Hot August Nights 178, 179
Hurst/Olds 130, 131
Hurst SC/Rambler 28, 29, 32

Impala 21, 43, 49, 62, 63, 64, 65
Indianapolis 500 42, 59
Iola Old Car Show 179

Javelin 25, 30, 31

Malibu 66, 67
Marauder 124, 125
Monte Carlo 68, 69
movies 9, 21, 53, 55, 65, 79, 103, 111, 173
Mustang 6, 9, 12, 20, 22, 50, 76, 90, 91, 92, 93, 100, 101, 102, 103, 104, 105, 107, 116, 158, 172, 173, 180, 181, 182, 184

NASCAR 46, 47, 49, 51, 66, 68, 69, 80, 81, 83, 96, 97, 98, 110, 112, 123, 124, 125, 140, 141, 147, 148, 149, 156, 157, 166, 175
Nova 8, 43, 70, 71

pace car 27, 59

rally racing 71
Rebel 25, 32, 33
Richard Petty 147, 148, 149, 175
Road Runner 86, 135, 144, 145, 148

Satellite 146, 147
Shelby Mustang 6, 104, 105, 107, 182
Skylark 34, 35, 36, 40, 41, 54
Super Bee 22, 86, 87, 88, 89
Superbird 134, 148, 149

Talladega 81, 110, 112, 113, 148
television shows 21, 53, 58, 65, 103, 111, 173
Thunderbird 108, 109, 110, 111, 164
Torino 81, 91, 112, 113, 114, 115, 148
Toronado 127, 132, 133
Torque 67
Trans Am 19, 51, 160, 162

unibody 94

V-8 4, 5, 6, 14, 17, 18, 28, 35, 36, 42, 43, 44, 45, 48, 49, 56, 57, 61, 62, 67, 70, 71, 74, 75, 76, 78, 84, 89, 101, 104, 105, 106, 107, 108, 114, 116, 118, 120, 122, 124, 125, 126, 136, 138, 141, 144, 146, 147, 156, 157, 159, 160, 166, 181
Valiant 136, 138, 150, 151
Ventura 170, 171

Woodward Dream Cruise 178, 179

PHOTO CREDITS

Cover Photos: Steve Lagreca/Dreamstime.com, front (group of cars); Zelfit/Shutterstock, front (V-8 Engine); Tohid Hashemkhani/Shutterstock, front (wrenches); Yevgen Belich/Shutterstock, front (red Chevrolet Corvette Stingray); Martina Birnbaum/Shutterstock, front (blue Ford Mustang); Raytags/Dreamstime.com, front (white AMC Rebel Machine with blue stripe); Gestalt Imagery/Shutterstock, front (red Chevrolet Chevelle with black stripes); Mike Windle/Getty Images Entertainment/Getty Images, front (black Pontiac Firebird Trans Am); Kylosova Maria/Shutterstock, front (yellow Chevrolet Camaro with black stripes); Goona14/Dreamstime.com, front (purple Dodge Charger); Calvin L. Leake/Dreamstime.com, front (Chevrolet Nova SS with flames; Brian Sullivan/Dreamstime.com, back (blue Chevrolet Corvette Stingray); Oleg Kovalenko/Dreamstime.com, back (red Ford Thunderbird)
Interior Photos: Oleg Kovalenko/Dreamstime.com, 1 (left), 14–15, 54–55, 120, 154–155; The Image Engine/Shutterstock, 1 (middle), 56; Raytags/Dreamstime.com, 1 (right), 7, 22 (bottom), 23 (top), 23 (bottom), 27, 32–33, 37, 38, 52, 72, 73, 76–77, 84–85, 119, 123 (top), 148–149, 174; Kevin Tichenor/Shutterstock, 2–3, 101; Gestalt Imagery/Shutterstock, 4–5, 12 (top left), 21 (middle), 50–51, 60–61, 124, 158, 168–169; Steve Lagreca/Dreamstime.com, 5, 100, 122, 130, 156, 159 (bottom), 178–179; Michael Cole/Corbis Sport/Getty Images, 6; Bruce Alan Bennett/Shutterstock, 8; Silver Screen Collection/Moviepix/Getty Images, 9; Universal History Archive/Universal Images Group/Getty Images, 10–11, 13 (bottom); Ruud Onos/Flickr, 12 (top middle); SvetlanaSF/iStock Editorial/Getty Images, 12 (bottom); MaxyM/Shutterstock, 13 (top); Pathompong Thongsan/iStock/Getty Images, 16; AM-C/E+/Getty Images, 17; alexluckyguy/Shutterstock, 18; chorche de prigo/Shutterstock, 18–19, 113, 159 (top), 170; Brphoto/Dreamstime.com, 20 (top), 34–35; StanRohrer/iStock/Getty Images, 20 (bottom); dolah/E+/Getty Images, 21 (top); Sue Thatcher/Shutterstock, 21 (bottom), 102–103; Dmitry Eagle Orlov/Shutterstock, 22 (top); National Motor Museum/Heritage Images/Hulton Archive/Getty Images, 22 (middle), 111, 134; Greg Gjerdingen/Wikimedia Commons, 23 (middle), 28–29, 86, 89 (bottom), 114–115 (top), 132, 142, 162–163; Calvin L. Leake/Dreamstime.com, 24, 70–71; Antonio Gumm/Dreamstime.com, 24–25; CZmarlin/Christopher Ziemnowicz/Wikimedia Commons, 26; Darren Dwayne Frazier/Dreamstime.com, 30–31; Brian Welker/Dreamstime.com, 33, 140, 152 (bottom left), 156–157, 171; Cars Down Under/Flickr, 36, 88, 116, 117, 142–143, 164; Barrett-Jackson/Getty Images, 39, 166–167; Bartus Daniel/Shutterstock, 40–41; Bettmann/Getty Images, 42, 118; Yevgen Belich/Shutterstock, 43; Leena Robinson/Shutterstock, 44; Michael Eldridge/Dreamstime.com, 45; Paulklee1879/Dreamstime.com, 46; betto rodrigues/Shutterstock, 46–47; RacingOne/ISC Archives/Getty Images, 47, 81, 110 (bottom), 112, 175; Steve Lagreca/Shutterstock, 48–49, 82–83, 187; Kylosova Maria/Shutterstock, 52–53; rzulev/Shutterstock, 53 (top); Jev pandev/Shutterstock, 53 (bottom); Brian Sullivan/Dreamstime.com, 57; kenmo/iStock Editorial/Getty Images, 58; Michael Allio/Icon Sportswire/Getty Images, 59; Heath Missen/iStock/Getty Images, 60; Jürgen Bierlein/Pixabay, 62; schlol/E+/Getty Images, 62–63, 128–129, 176–177; Mediagia/Dreamstime.com, 64–65; Peeler37/Dreamstime.com, 66; Vauxford/Wikimedia Commons, 67; Allen Kee/WireImage/Getty Images, 68; Barry Blackburn/Shutterstock, 69; Johann68/Dreamstime.com, 70, 151; VanderWolfImages/Dreamstime.com, 74–75; Gilles Malo/Dreamstime.com, 75; Goona14/Dreamstime.com, 78; Edaldridge/Dreamstime.com, 79 (top); Sicnag/Wikimedia Commons, 79 (bottom), 97; Hans Koster/Dreamstime.com, 80; Darryl Norenberg/The Enthusiast Network/Getty Images, 82; Randy Gauthier/Shutterstock, 87; Cjp24/Wikimedia Commons, 89 (top); Hulton Archive/Getty Images, 90; Milos Ruzicka/iStock Editorial/Getty Images, 91; Wirestock Creators/Shutterstock, 92; Dan74/Shutterstock, 93; kontrast-fotodesign/iStock Unreleased/Getty Images, 94; Michel Curi/Flickr, 95, 139; Eli Christman/Flickr, 96; Triple-green/Auge=mit/Wikimedia Commons, 98–99; Radu Bercan/Shutterstock, 103; Don Heiny/The Image Bank Unreleased/Getty Images, 104; pasicevo/Shutterstock, 105; Bernard Cahier/Hulton Archive/Getty Images, 106; Sigurbjornragnarsson/Dreamstime.com, 106–107, 135, 144–145, 182; GPS 56/Flickr, 108, 146, 181; Vadim Rodnev/Shutterstock, 109; BoJack/Shutterstock, 110 (top); Mike Kemp/Corbis Historical/Getty Images, 114–115 (bottom); Ldionisio/Dreamstime.com, 121 (top); Pat Brollier/The Enthusiast Network/Getty Images, 121 (bottom); CTRPhotos/iStock Editorial/Getty Images, 123 (bottom); xiao car/Flickr, 125; Whiteaster/Shutterstock, 126; allanw/Shutterstock, 127; omersukrugoksu/iStock Unreleased/Getty Images, 129; Jeffrey S Downes/Dreamstime.com, 131; Phonlamai Photo/Shutterstock, 133; MercurySable99/Wikimedia Commons, 136; Anton Sokolov/Dreamstime.com, 136–137; Kevauto/Wikimedia Commons, 138; MAXSHOT.PL/Shutterstock, 141; Tony Savino/Dreamstime.com, 144; Zach Catanzareti Photo/Flickr, 146–147; Different_Brian/iStock Editorial/Getty Images, 150; General Motors Company/Wikimedia Commons, 152 (bottom right); Ron Kimball/Kimball Stock, 153; Iv-olga/Shutterstock, 160; Mike Windle/Getty Images Entertainment/Getty Images, 161; Rex Gray/Flickr, 165; Photo Spirit/Shutterstock, 172; Johnnie Rik/Shutterstock, 173; Gary Leonard/Corbis Historical/Getty Images, 177; Thank You (21 Millions+) views/Prayitno Photography/Flickr, 178; Brett Levin/Flickr, 180; Cindy Haggerty/Shutterstock, 183 (top); Chris Bence/Shutterstock, 183 (bottom); tomeng/iStock Unreleased/Getty Images, 184 (top); Kai Lehmann/Wikimedia Commons, 184 (bottom); JDzacovsky/Shutterstock, 185 (top); Raymond Boyd/Michael Ochs Archives/Getty Images, 185 (bottom); Erik Cox Photography/Shutterstock, 186

ABDOBOOKS.COM

Published by Abdo Reference, a division of ABDO, PO Box 398166, Minneapolis, Minnesota 55439. Copyright © 2025 by Abdo Consulting Group, Inc. International copyrights reserved in all countries. No part of this book may be reproduced in any form without written permission from the publisher. Encyclopedias™ is a trademark and logo of Abdo Reference.

Printed in China
092024
012025

THIS BOOK CONTAINS RECYCLED MATERIALS

Editor: Carrie Hasler
Series Designer: Colleen McLaren

LIBRARY OF CONGRESS CONTROL NUMBER: 2023949485

PUBLISHER'S CATALOGING-IN-PUBLICATION DATA
Names: Russo, Kristin J., author.
Title: The muscle cars encyclopedia / by Kristin J. Russo
Description: Minneapolis, Minnesota : Abdo Reference, 2025 | Series: Motorsports encyclopedias | Includes online resources and index.
Identifiers: ISBN 9781098294434 (lib. bdg.) | ISBN 9798384913702 (ebook)
Subjects: LCSH: Motorsports--Juvenile literature. | Motor racing--Juvenile literature. | Automobile racing--Juvenile literature. | Muscle cars--Juvenile literature. | Races (Sports)--Juvenile literature. | Encyclopedias and dictionaries--Juvenile literature.
Classification: DDC 796.72--dc23